THE COOKING MOM

Delicious recipes, secrets, and stories from a real mom who can help bring your family back to the table.

By Amy Hanten

Cover photographs by Glenn Sanderson

ISBN: 0983035601
ISBN-13: 9780983035602

This book is dedicated to my husband and best friend, Bob,

and to our kids Riley and Ireland.

INDEX

BREAKFAST AND BRUNCH TIME 133

NO MORE BORING SANDWICHES 159

KICKED UP CASSEROLES 171

JUST THROW IT IN THE SLOW COOKER 201

WHAT'S FOR DINNER? I'M HUNGRY 221

I'M THIRSTY 335

Thank you

Wow, where do I start? How about at the beginning?

Thanks family. You know who you are and I love each and every one of you dearly!

Thanks mom and dad for letting me cook dinner and make a mess in the kitchen whenever I wanted to. Oh yeah, and thanks for buying all the groceries too! It's been more than twenty-five years since I left home for college and they are still finding weird stuff like capers in their cupboards. Yep, that was me. Thanks too for always supporting me and listening, no matter what!

Thanks to my sister and her husband Sean and their kids. Whenever we get together they put up with me taking over in the kitchen. Thanks guys for all the love and some great recipes too!

My grandmother, Corinne Golden, I called her Mimi, passed away not long ago. She was an amazing cook! She also threw one great party! Actually every night was a party at her house! I learned so much from her. Thanks for teaching me how to cook and entertain, Mimi. I think you'd really like this book!

Thanks friends. From my tennis gals to my co-workers, I treasure you all. I am so lucky to have you in my life! Susan, you have always, and I mean always, been there. We did it!

Thanks to the great gals at Bob's office, Jocelyn, Annette and Angie for the help with editing this monster. It's a big book! More than 250 recipes!

Thanks to everyone in Northeast Wisconsin who have been letting me into their living rooms and watching me on television for nearly twenty years. I'm not originally from here and never thought this is where I would settle down, but how could I leave? I've never met nicer, more genuine people! What a great place to raise a family. I am proud to call Green Bay, Wisconsin home. What's a little cold weather??

Thanks to all of the chefs and great cooks I've met along the way. I have learned so much from you. A lot of your recipes are in this book. Thank you!!

Finally a huge thank you to my immediate family! You rock! Thanks to my son, Riley who got me squared away on the computer so I could get started on this book. Trust me that was no easy task! To my daughter Ireland who always wants to be in the kitchen with me. If I'm "The Cooking Mom", she is "The Cooking Kid"!!! Thanks sweetie for always being so bright and sunny. Also for being so patient when they took the pictures for the book. Talk about a long day! You did great! Thank goodness for the cookie dough! Thanks to Levi, our huge Chocolate Lab. His tail is always wagging when I walk in the door at the end of a log day. Plus, he makes cleaning up the kitchen floor after I cook so much easier! And, Bob, what can I say? You know how I feel but I'll tell you anyway. I am so grateful you came into my life. Thank you for ALL you do! Love you guys!!

Introduction

It seems like I have always been into food. One of my earliest memories involves a pork chop! The postman rang the door bell. I went to open it with nothing but my birthday suit on and, a pork chop in my mouth. My mom was mortified! I was only two and I really do remember it.

The favorite foods listed in my baby book weren't the usual kid stuff. Instead it was London broil and red velvet cake. Told you I was a "foodie" really early on.

Both my parents worked so I was able to con them into letting me make dinner sometimes. I also did most of the grocery shopping. I LOVE to grocery shop and I always have. (I know, weird!) My poor parents would drop me off with a blank check and I would seriously load up that cart. I'd always get into a little trouble for spending too much. Okay, I deserved it!

I was one of those kids who pretty much always knew what they wanted to do. I wanted to be a broadcast journalist, you know one of those gals on the news. I was the editor of my grade school newspaper and loved it! I also did the school announcements every morning, so I was on my way!

My dream came true! I worked hard in college and got my Journalism degree from Marquette University. In college I was lucky enough to work at two Milwaukee T.V. stations so that I could really learn the ropes. Then, it was time to hit the road and get on T.V. myself. My first real on-air job was at a little station in Zanesville, Ohio. They hired me to do the weather. I knew NOTHING about the weather and I was bad, (okay really bad)!! But, they saw something in me and it wasn't long before I was anchoring the morning and noon news. I moved from there to a few different stations across the country, two in Iowa, and one in Omaha. Finally it was time for Bob and I to end our long-distance marriage. (Yep, we lived in separate cities our first year! How crazy is that?) We met in Wisconsin in college and really fell in love with it, so that's where we decided to settle down.

I've worked at WLUK Fox 11 in Green Bay for almost 20 years now. That's a long time in the crazy world of television. I started out anchoring a half hour morning news show and then before long it turned into a four hour show. I had to be there at 4 a.m. every morning.

(Trust me, that's really early!!) When, I first started there one of the producers asked me what kind of fun segments I could do on the show. I knew right away. Cooking! So, that's how it all started. I'd invite chefs to come on our morning show to cook with me. It was a blast, and people we're loving it. No one else was doing it in this market. Then, I thought, why can't I do some of the cooking segments myself, and so I did!

The rest is history. Two years ago the boss offered me my own cooking/lifestyle show. Are you kidding me? YES, YES, YES!! I get to cook and talk (which I do a lot of) everyday. It's one of the only, in fact it may be THE ONLY, live hour-long cooking shows in the country. Pretty cool! Anything can and does happen! From fires (yep we had a small one), to cuts (not me, my producer), oh yeah and lots of burned nuts! I always burn the nuts, at home and on the show! Oh well! Anyway, I am having the time of my life!

I can't tell you how many times I've been asked, "When's the cookbook coming out?" Well, here it is. I call myself "The Cooking Mom". I am no chef, just a busy mom who's trying my best to get my family to the table. No, not every night. I think those days sadly are gone! My mission is to try and help other busy folks like me. I get it! I'm in the trenches too! It's a crazy, busy world out there so we've got to hang together. Eating together is so darn important! My kids grumble when I say "family dinner tonight." But, the next thing you know we're all talking and laughing and connecting. No computer or cell phones! LOVE IT! If my family can do it, yours can too!

My recipes are easy and they are really good! I am the self-proclaimed "Queen of Casseroles!" I love them! Why, because the ones I make taste great and they make getting dinner on the table easy! Same goes for my slow cooker! There's a whole chapter filled with amazing casserole recipes and one on slow cooker recipes too! I think you'll dig it! Many of my all-time favorite and most requested recipes are in here. I've also gotten some great recipes from the chefs and wonderful people I've met along the way. You'll see some of their recipes in here too.

I had to end somewhere so if you don't see one of your favorite recipes in here, maybe it will be in the next book. I can't believe I'm even saying that! I hope it gets to the point where the pages get stuck together and there are lots of food stains all over this book. That's what happens to my favorite cookbooks! Sure hope it happens to this one too! Now, get cookin' and bring that family of yours together!

Secrets from The Cooking Mom

I have not eaten greasy fast food in, I promise you, 16 years. I still remember that bad stomach ache after hitting the drive-thru for dinner. Never again! Yes, my kids still eat it every once in awhile. Come on, they're kids.

Anyway, I try really hard to have a home cooked dinner on the table every night. Not that we eat together every night, we don't. I'm happy if we can eat together at least three times a week. Always on a Sunday. That seems to help get the week off to the right start. Then maybe on one or two other weeknights, when everybody's schedules mesh and we can make it happen. If it's a crazy week, don't sweat it. Maybe it can happen next week. Just try! That's all you can do. And, make sure to give everybody a heads up as to when you're having family dinner night. That way you can count on the whole gang to show up.

Just like the football teams do, put a game plan together. I usually sit down with a cup of coffee and the ads in the Sunday paper and get inspired. What's on sale this week? What's in season? What am I in the mood for? I pick one main ingredient, like beef, chicken or pork. Then, I see what I've got in my pantry and in my fridge. Now it's time to go shopping. I don't do lists. I probably should. I used to but then I'd always forget the list at home anyway.

I plan one big "Cooking Day". Usually on a Sunday. Now, we're not talking all day. Just an hour or two. If it's chicken, instead of baking 4 chicken breasts, I'll bake up 8 or 12. My secret way to cook them is coming up on the next page. Then, I'll use those chicken breasts in casseroles or soups. Same goes for a roast. I'll do a couple roasts or one big one in the slow cooker and use the leftovers to make enchiladas and soups. You get it now. Cook once, get 3 to 4 different meals out of it. Once you get the hang of it, you'll see. It really works! Saves time and a lot of money too!!

Also, remember you don't have to do it all! Don't try and be Super Mom or Dad! It will catch up to you! Most groceries stores rock these days! Pick up dessert! Pick up some great bread! Hit the deli. Pick up some twice baked potatoes to go with that steak. Just make one or two things and take help where you can get it!

I love rotisserie chickens! My mom got me hooked on them years ago. Instead of hitting the drive-thru, pick up one of those warm golden juicy chickens. Costs less and is so much better for you than greasy burgers. Use the leftovers in soups and casseroles.

Don't be scared to invite people over. Everything doesn't have to be perfect! Some of my best times happen not at a fancy restaurant but at my dining room table with family and friends. If someone asks you what they can bring. Don't saying "nothing"! They're going to bring something anyway. It might as well be something you can use. If it's a friend who likes to bake, ask them to bring dessert. If it's someone like my friend Susan, who's a busy lady and doesn't cook much, ask them to pick up dessert or a veggie and dip tray, or bring a bottle of wine. Trust me real friends appreciate straight shooters.

Keep a well stocked pantry if you can. Watch for sales and stock up on things like pasta, canned vegetables, canned cream soups, tuna, rice, and beans. My freezer always is stocked with chicken breasts and ground beef. And of course all the baking stuff too, like sugar and flour and all that jazz. I try to keep a few boxed cake mixes on hand too, just in case. "I need cupcakes for school tomorrow!" We've all heard that before. It makes life so much easier when you don't have to make that last minute run to the grocery store at the end of a long day!

Lastly, turn on some tunes during dinner. Not too loud. We do it all the time! We love the standards in our house. I think it's gotten the kids to fall in love with music other than the Top 40 stuff. I really believe that music makes every meal and every party even better. Except if it's a picnic at the beach. Then I just want to hear the birds and the waves.

My Secret Way to Bake Chicken Breasts

4 to 12 or even more boneless, skinless chicken breasts halves

A couple tablespoons of olive oil

Garlic salt and pepper

Large sheet of heavy-duty foil (not the cheap stuff)

Preheat the oven to 350 degrees. Line up the chicken in a row on the foil. Drizzle each piece with a little olive oil. Season each piece with some salt and pepper. Wrap up the foil (not too tight) to make a packet. Place packet on a jelly roll pan. Bake for 40 to 55 minutes depending on your oven and how many pieces of chicken you're cooking. Remove from the oven and let cool for about ten minutes. Carefully open the foil packet. There you go chicken, lots of chicken for the whole week.

∞ ∞ ∞

This is by far my most requested recipe. Need chicken for soups or casseroles. This is the way I do it. The chicken stays moist and it's so easy. Clean-up is a breeze too! LOVE THAT! I think doing it this way gives the chicken so much more flavor than boiling it. Season it however you want. I LOVE my garlic salt! Regular salt works just fine too. If you're using it an Italian recipe you can season the chicken with some dried Italian seasoning too. Mexican? Throw a little cumin and chili powder on top. I usually just stick with the garlic salt and pepper. That way it works in anything I feel like making. Hey, one more thing. Shred or dice up the chicken while it's still warm. It's easier to work with that way!

∞ ∞ ∞

MUNCHIES

SNACKS

AND APPETIZERS

My Weakness!

Mimi's Crab Dip

1 package (8 ounces) cream cheese, softened

1 tablespoon milk

1/2 teaspoon garlic salt

1 teaspoon Worcestershire sauce

2 teaspoons lemon juice

2/3 cup chili sauce

1 can (4.25 ounces) crab meat, drained well

2 tablespoons fresh chopped Italian parsley

Use a mixer and beat together the first five ingredients together until smooth. Spread into a dish or pie plate. Spread chili sauce over top of cream cheese mixture. Spoon crab meat over the chili sauce. Sprinkle with parsley. Cover loosely and refrigerate a few hours before serving. Serve chilled with crackers. Best if eaten that day!

൶ ൶ ൶

My grandmother, Mimi, was a great cook who loved entertaining. I learned so much from her. Cocktails and snacks were an every night thing at her summer cottage on Walloon Lake in Michigan. When people stopped by while boating, she was always ready. The kitchen in the cottage was tiny but it didn't matter. Mimi cooked some of the best meals I've ever eaten. I had to start this book with one of her recipes. Everybody loved this dip. I still do! Miss you Mimi, but think of you all the time!

൶ ൶ ൶

∽ ∽ ∽

Here's my grandmother, Mimi. She passed away recently at the age of 91 but she's with me every day in the kitchen. What a great cook! Every night was a party at her house! What great times!

∽ ∽ ∽

My Favorite Shrimp Spread

1 stick butter, softened

1 package (8 ounces) cream cheese, softened

1 tablespoon fresh lemon juice

1/4 cup mayonnaise

Dash of hot sauce

1 teaspoon garlic salt

1/4 pound cooked shrimp, diced

2 tablespoons scallions, chopped

In a food processor or using a mixer mix together first six ingredients until smooth. Mix in shrimp and scallions. Chill for a few hours before serving. Serve with crackers. Keeps in the fridge for up to 3 days.

ɲ ɲ ɲ

This is a great way to serve shrimp without spending a ton of money. Everybody loves it! We serve it as a starter at our annual summer seafood boil. Keeps people happy until dinner's ready.

ɲ ɲ ɲ

Spinach Dip in a Bread Bowl

1 package (10 ounces) frozen chopped spinach, thawed and squeezed dry

1 container (16 ounces) sour cream

1 cup mayonnaise

1 envelope dry vegetable soup mix

1 can (8 ounces) water chestnuts, drained

3 scallions chopped

1 round loaf crusty sourdough or pumpernickel bread, unsliced

1 to 2 loaves crusty French or sourdough bread

Combine first 6 ingredients in a big bowl. Cover well and chill for two hours or overnight. When ready to serve cut the top off and hollow out the round loaf of bread to form a bowl. Spoon dip into the bread bowl. Cut the bread you scooped out of the bowl into chunks. Slice the other loaf of bread into bite size pieces. Serve bread bowl on a big platter surrounded by the bread cubes for dipping. Also great with fresh veggies for dipping.

∽ ∽ ∽

What can I say? It's just a classic. I thought everybody had this recipe but every time I make it for a party people ask me for it, so here it is.

∽ ∽ ∽

Swiss Pecan Dip

1 cup finely shredded Swiss cheese

2 scallions, finely chopped

1¼ cup mayonnaise

1/2 cup chopped pecans

1/2 teaspoon seasoning salt

Mix everything together. Cover and refrigerate for at least two hours before serving. Serve with your favorite crackers. I like it with Triscuits.

∾ ∾ ∾

My good friend Deb's mother-in-law gave me this recipe. It's really rich, so try to keep yourself from eating too much, but man, is it good! Thanks Lenore!

∾ ∾ ∾

Layered Mexican Dip

1 can (16 ounces) refried beans

1 envelope (1.25 ounces) taco seasoning

1 cup sour cream

1 jar (16 ounces) chunky salsa

2 cups shredded iceberg lettuce

2 cups shredded Mexican blend cheese

1 can (2.25 ounces) sliced black olives

1/2 cup tomatoes, seeded and diced

1/4 cup scallions, finely diced

In a bowl mix together refried beans with the taco seasoning. Spread mixture on the bottom of a medium sized casserole dish. Then layer on the sour cream, salsa, lettuce, cheese, olives, tomatoes and scallions. Refrigerate until ready to serve. Best eaten the same day. Serve with tortilla chips for dipping.

∾ ∾ ∾

This is a great game day recipe. I have to thank Green Bay Packers' wife, Andrea Collins, the woman behind Nick Collins, for this one. She made it for me on my show and I've been making it ever since. I added more cheese and tomatoes. Gotta have more cheese, right?

∾ ∾ ∾

Layered Greek Dip

1 package (8 ounces) cream cheese, softened

2 tablespoons milk

1 tablespoon lemon juice

1 teaspoon dried Italian seasoning

2 cloves garlic, minced

1/2 teaspoon garlic salt

1 container (10 ounces) of hummus or 1¼ cup homemade hummus

1 cup cucumber, seeded and diced

1 cup tomato, seeded and diced

1/2 cup pitted kalamata olives, chopped

1/2 cup crumbled feta cheese

1/3 cup scallions, chopped

Pita chips

In a bowl, beat cream cheese, milk, lemon juice, Italian seasoning, garlic salt and garlic with electric mixer for a few minutes until smooth. Spread cream cheese mixture into a 9" pie plate or shallow serving dish. Evenly, spread hummus over cream cheese layer. Top with cucumber, tomato, olives, feta and scallions. Cover and refrigerate for at least an hour before serving. Best if served within 4 to 6 hours. Serve chilled with pita chips.

∿ ∿ ∿

This is a really yummy dip recipe and something different! The cream cheese is layered with the hummus and then all those fun toppings. Really cool and fresh to serve with those great tomatoes and cucumbers in the summer! And don't worry about making your own hummus. I always say, "You can't do it all!" But, if you want to, I've got a great recipe for it on the next page.

∿ ∿ ∿

Hummus

2 cans (15 ounces) garbanzo beans or chick peas, drained

1/4 cup tahini (ground sesame seeds in a jar)

2 tablespoons fresh lemon juice

1 teaspoon salt

2 cloves garlic

2 scallions, chopped

1/4 cup olive oil, plus 1 to 2 tablespoons for drizzling on top

1/2 teaspoon paprika

2 tablespoons fresh chopped Italian parsley

Place first 7 ingredients in a food processor. Pulse until smooth. Transfer mixture to a serving bowl or plate. Drizzle olive oil over the hummus. Sprinkle with paprika and parsley. Serve with warm pita bread and fresh veggies for dipping.

∽ ∽ ∽

A pretty much guilt-free dip! Bob and I love it! Serve this with some assorted olives and some chunks of feta cheese, and I'm a happy camper!

∽ ∽ ∽

Dill Dip

1 cup mayonnaise

1 cup sour cream

1 tablespoon dried minced onion

1 teaspoon dried parsley flakes

1 tablespoon dried dill weed

1 teaspoon Beau Monde Seasoning or garlic salt

Mix all ingredients well. Keep refrigerated until ready to serve. Makes 2 cups. Serve with lots of raw vegetables for dipping. Keeps in the fridge for up to a week.

∾ ∾ ∾

I got this recipe years ago from one of the head chefs at Lambeau Field. It was the dip they served on all those veggie trays to those lucky folks in the luxury boxes. Not me, I'm in the cheap seats! Anyway, we eat this dip all summer long on our porch. It is so easy, and a great way to get the kids to eat veggies. I love it with cucumbers, carrots, celery, sliced red pepper, and broccoli. By the way, Beau Monde Seasoning is a blend with celery, onion, garlic and some other stuff. If you can't find it, just use garlic salt.

∾ ∾ ∾

Fruit Dip

1 package (8 ounces) softened cream cheese

1 container (7 ounces) marshmallow crème

1 tablespoon fresh orange juice

1 teaspoon fresh orange zest

Use a mixer and beat together all ingredients until smooth. Refrigerate for a couple of hours. Serve chilled with fresh fruit for dipping.

∾ ∾ ∾

Want the kids to eat more fruit? Make this dip! It's so good you can even get away with serving this for dessert! It's a summertime favorite with fresh strawberries. Yum! Thanks to my dear friend and second mom, Susie, for this one.

∾ ∾ ∾

Beer Dip

2 packages (8 ounces) cream cheese, softened

1/4 cup beer (somebody gets to drink the rest!)

1 packet (1 ounce) dry ranch dip mix

1½ cups finely shredded cheddar cheese

With a mixer beat together cream cheese, dip mix and beer until smooth. Stir in cheese and chill for at least 2 hours. Serve chilled with pretzels.

∾ ∾ ∾

We try to figure out a way to put beer in everything in Wisconsin! This dip gets gobbled up at my football parties. I got the recipe from a serious tailgater who never misses a Packers game, no matter what the weather. It's great with the seasoned pretzels recipe coming up later in this chapter.

∾ ∾ ∾

Yooper Cheese Spread

2 packages (8 ounces) cream cheese, softened

2 containers (8 ounces) cold pack sharp cheddar cheese spread

1/4 cup milk

1/4 cup grated parmesan cheese

1 teaspoon garlic powder

1 teaspoon beef soup base (paste, not powder or cubes)

2 teaspoons Worcestershire sauce

A few dashes of hot sauce

With a food processor or hand mixer, mix together all ingredients until smooth. Refrigerate for at least a few hours before serving. Great with crackers or warm breadsticks. Keeps in the fridge for at least a week.

∾ ∾ ∾

Ever been to Marquette, Michigan? What a cool town! Great skiing in the winter! What a view from Marquette Mountain! Anyway, after skiing folks warm up with a cocktail and cheese spread served with warm garlic bread sticks. An Upper Peninsula or as we call it, "U.P." tradition. Gotta love dose "Yoopers!"

∾ ∾ ∾

Cheddar Cheese Ball

1 package (8 ounces) cream cheese, softened

1 container (8 ounces) cold pack sharp cheddar cheese

2 teaspoons Worcestershire sauce

Dash hot sauce

1 teaspoon garlic powder

1 jar (2 ounces) chopped pimento drained

2 tablespoons diced scallions

1/2 cup fresh Italian parsley, finely chopped

1/2 cup red pepper, finely diced

Plastic wrap

In a food processor or with a mixer, mix together first five ingredients until smooth. Mix in scallions and pimento. Cover and refrigerate for a few hours or overnight. Place cheese mixture on a large piece of plastic wrap to form ball. Roll cheese ball in parsley and red pepper. Chill until ready to serve. Serve on a plate surrounded by crackers.

෴ ෴ ෴

It's "CHEESEBALL CENTRAL" in Wisconsin. Every party has to have one. Homemade ones are so much better than the pre-made ones. You don't even want to know what's in those! Anyway, I love cheese balls because they look pretty and you can totally make them ahead of time. This cheddar ball is a classic but you'll see some more of my cheese ball favorites on the next few pages. The key to a good cheese ball is to make it a day or two ahead so it has to time to set up and you can form it into a ball. So go ahead, get cheesy!

෴ ෴ ෴

Disappearing Olive Cheese Ball

1 package (8 ounces) cream cheese, softened

1/2 teaspoon celery salt

1/2 teaspoon garlic powder

1/4 teaspoon onion powder

1 can (4.25 ounces) chopped black olives

1/2 cup finely shredded cheddar cheese

1/2 cup chopped, toasted pecans

Using a mixer or food processor combine first 4 ingredients until smooth. Stir in olives and cheese. Refrigerate for a few hours or overnight. Place mixture on a sheet of plastic wrap. Shape into a ball and roll in the pecans. Chill until ready to serve. Serve on a platter surrounded by crackers.

ഗ ഗ ഗ

This one always disappears! I am a huge fan of olives!! Recipe is from my friend John from Milwaukee. Thanks John!

ഗ ഗ ഗ

Bleu Cheese Ball

1 package (8 ounces) cheese, softened

1/2 cup crumbled bleu cheese

2 tablespoons chopped scallions

A few dashes hot sauce

1/2 cup Italian parsley, finely chopped

1/2 cup chopped walnuts, toasted

Mix first 4 ingredients in food processor and chill for a few hours or overnight or until firm. Place the cheese mixture on a large sheet of plastic wrap and form into a ball. Roll in parsley and then nuts. Refrigerate until ready to serve. Serve on a plate surrounded by crackers.

∾ ∾ ∾

Not a big bleu cheese fan. I get it! But, I still think you'll like this one. The cream cheese mellows it out a bit. I love the combination of bleu cheese and walnuts! This one is a winner!!

∾ ∾ ∾

Football Cheese Ball

2 packages (8 ounces) cream cheese, softened

1 package (8 ounces) shredded sharp cheddar cheese

1/2 cup grated Parmesan cheese

1/2 cup mayonnaise

2 teaspoons Worcestershire sauce

1 teaspoon garlic powder

1/4 teaspoon pepper

2 scallions, chopped

1/4 cup real bacon bits or pieces

1 cup chopped pecans

Pimento or roasted red pepper slices

Beat first 8 ingredients with mixer or in food processor until blended. Stir in scallions and bacon. Refrigerate several hours or overnight. Form into football shape, coat with nuts to get the brown color of a football. Cut pimento or red pepper into thin strips and use to form laces of football on top. Serve on a platter surrounded with crackers. If you don't like nuts you can also use more bacon bits to make it look like a football.

∿ ∿ ∿

We love football in Wisconsin! Anytime we can have people over to watch a game and snack we do. This cheese football is really good and it's so cute that it can even double as a centerpiece for your spread! Better take a picture because it will be gone before you know it! Thanks to my dear friend, Christine, for this one. She makes everybody happy!!

∿ ∿ ∿

Texas Caviar

2 cans (15 ounces) black eyed peas, drained and rinsed

2 cans (10 ounces) shoe peg corn, drained

2 cans (15 ounces) black beans, drained and rinsed

1 cup red onion, finely diced

1½ cups green pepper, finely diced

2 to 4 jalapeno peppers, finely chopped (optional)

4 Roma tomatoes, seeded and diced

2 ripe avocados, diced (optional)

1 cup cilantro, chopped

1 bottle (12 ounces) zesty Italian dressing

Mix all ingredients, except avocado, in a large bowl. Cover and refrigerate until ready to serve. Add avocados just before serving. Serve with tortilla chips or scoops.

ᘐ ᘐ ᘐ

People can't stop eating this. It's just so good! I love the avocado in this but if you don't, no big deal, just leave it out. This is great in the summer. It's also a great game day starter before tacos or chili at half time. Serve it with baked chips and it's pretty much guilt-free. Okay, I like the regular tortilla chips way better! This caviar is way less expensive than the real stuff, which kind of creeps me out! Fish eggs, really? I'll stick with this stuff.

ᘐ ᘐ ᘐ

Great Guacamole

2 ripe avocados

3 tablespoons diced red onion

1 jalapeno pepper, stems and seeds removed, finely diced (optional)

3 tablespoons cilantro leaves, finely chopped

Juice from half a lime

1/2 teaspoon salt

1/2 cup ripe tomatoes, seeded and diced

Using a fork or potato masher, mash the avocados. Add remaining ingredients. Add more salt if needed. Serve right away with tortilla chips.   You really can't make this ahead of time. Make it and eat it right away!

ಌ ಌ ಌ

Keep it simple. That's what makes great guacamole. This is how they do it in Mexico. Most places make it right at your table. I've been lucky enough to go there a few times. My friend Carmen, who's from Mexico, tipped me off about using a potato masher to mash the avocados. It works great! If you can't get to Mexico, make this and a pitcher of margaritas and it's the next best thing, well kind of!

ಌ ಌ ಌ

Tortilla Roll Ups

1 cup sour cream

2 packages (8 ounces) cream cheese

1 can (4.25 ounces) chopped black olives

1 can (4 ounces) chopped green chilies

1½ cups finely shredded cheddar cheese

1 packet (1ounce) dry ranch dressing mix

8 to 10 (10") flour tortillas

Salsa for dipping

Use a mixer to mix cream cheese, sour cream and ranch mix until smooth. By hand, stir in olives, chilies and cheese. Spread a thin layer on tortillas and roll up. Wrap each tightly in plastic wrap. Refrigerate for at least a few hours. When ready to serve, slice roll ups into 1 inch pieces. Serve with salsa for dipping.

෨ ෨ ෨

I can't get enough of these! Neither can anyone else, so make plenty! You might want to double the recipe! Plus, you can make them ahead of your party. LOVE THAT! My sister Cary and her husband Sean made these for me once and I was hooked! A great starter to my "Super Simple White Chicken Chili" recipe coming up in the "Soup's On" chapter later in the book.

෨ ෨ ෨

Olive Tapenade

1½ cups kalamata olives, pitted

2 garlic cloves

1/4 cup fresh Italian parsley leaves

1/4 teaspoon dried oregano

1/4 teaspoon red pepper

1/4 cup extra virgin olive oil

2 tablespoons capers

In a food processor combine first 5 ingredients.   Pulse a few times. Add the oil and capers and pulse twice. Store tightly covered in the refrigerator. This will keep in the fridge for up to a week. Serve with crackers or with crusty bread.

∾ ∾ ∾

Company coming over at the last minute? No worries! This takes minutes to whip up. Why buy the pre-made stuff in the jar when you can make your own in minutes and it's so much better!!! It's great on an antipasto platter with assorted olives, Italian cheeses and Italian meats. Don't have a food processor, no big deal, just chop everything up by hand.

∾ ∾ ∾

Sundried Tomato Dip

1 package (8 ounces) cream cheese, softened

1/2 cup mayonnaise

1/2 cup sour cream

Dash hot sauce

1/2 teaspoon garlic salt

1/4 cup sundried tomatoes, packed in oil and drained

2 scallions, chopped

Put the first 5 ingredients in a food processor. Pulse until smooth. Add tomatoes and scallions. Pulse a couple times. You should be able to see some pieces of tomato and scallion. Chill for a few hours before serving. Great with crackers or fresh vegetables.

❧ ❧ ❧

Every time I make this dip people beg me for the recipe. It's so quick and easy. Keep a jar of sundried tomatoes in your pantry and some cream cheese in the fridge and you're good to go! My gal pals love this. Sometimes we'll put a big platter together with this dip, a bowl of my olive tapenade (recipe's on the previous page), some sliced Italian meats and cheeses, some crackers and bread and call it dinner. Now that's a good time!!!

❧ ❧ ❧

Melon and Prosciutto

2 tablespoons sherry or white wine vinegar

1 tablespoon honey

1 teaspoon fresh thyme

1/4 cup olive oil

Salt and pepper

1 ripe cantaloupe

1/2 pound prosciutto, thinly sliced (ask for it at the deli, if they don't have it you can use thinly sliced good ham)

Whisk together first 4 ingredients. Season with a little salt and pepper. Slice melon into thin wedges and cut 3/4 of the way between skin and flesh. Wrap prosciutto around cut pieces of melon. Drizzle a little of the vinaigrette on top right before serving.

∾ ∾ ∾

I can't take credit for this one. I got this recipe from celebrity chef Tyler Florence. What a nice guy (and cute too)! We had a chance to work together a few years ago and he literally swept me off my feet!

∾ ∾ ∾

∾ ∾ ∾ ∾

Celebrity Chef and Food Network Star Tyler Florence swept me off my feet! I had the chance to work with him when he came to Green Bay a couple years ago. Super nice guy!

∾ ∾ ∾ ∾

Beer-Boiled Shrimp

1 cup water

2 bottles (12 ounces) beer

2 Bay leaves

1 tablespoon whole black peppercorns

2 teaspoons celery seed

2 cloves garlic, peeled

2 to 3 pounds shrimp

2 lemons

Combine water, beer, garlic, a few slices of lemon and seasonings in a large pan and bring to a boil over high heat. Add shrimp. Cover; remove from heat and let stand 5 to 8 minutes or just until shrimp turn pink. Drain and chill shrimp. Serve shrimp chilled with cocktail sauce and lemon wedges.

∽ ∽ ∽

Like shrimp cocktail? Don't buy the pre-cooked stuff! Boil it yourself. It's got so much more flavor! Just make sure you have plenty if you are serving it at a party. It's the first thing to go! Gotta serve it with "Seriously Good Shrimp Cocktail Sauce." That recipe is on the next page.

∽ ∽ ∽

Seriously Good Shrimp Cocktail Sauce

1 bottle (12 ounces) chili sauce

1½ cups ketchup

A few dashes of hot sauce

1 tablespoon Worcestershire sauce

1/2 cup prepared horseradish

1 small lemon, zest & juice

Combine all the ingredients in a large bowl and whisk until thoroughly mixed. Refrigerate until ready to serve. Keeps for up to a week in the fridge. Serve cold with shrimp cocktail. If you want it a little less spicy back off on the horseradish. Man, this stuff is good!

∿ ∿ ∿

If you're making shrimp cocktail, you HAVE to make this sauce! It rocks! It's got a little kick to it, but it's supposed to. Thanks to my friend, Chef Abbey, for this one!

∿ ∿ ∿

Spinach and Artichoke Dip

1 (10 ounce) package frozen chopped spinach, thawed, drained and squeezed dry

1 can (14 ounces) quartered artichoke hearts, drained and chopped

2 cloves garlic, minced

1 cup mayonnaise

1 (8 ounce) package cream cheese, softened

2 tablespoons lemon juice

3/4 cup grated parmesan cheese

1 cup shredded mozzarella cheese

Preheat oven to 350 degrees. Spray a small casserole dish with cooking spray. In a medium bowl, mix together the cream cheese and mayonnaise until smooth. Mix in artichoke hearts, spinach and both cheeses. Stir in garlic and lemon juice. Spread into the baking dish. Bake uncovered for 15 to 25 minutes until brown and bubbly. Serve warm out of the oven with crackers or sliced French bread for dipping.

∽ ∽ ∽

This dip, a good movie, and Bob sitting next to me on the couch. Doesn't take much to make me happy! Oh yeah and Levi, the dog, at our feet! Life is good!!! (Unless the movie is *Braveheart*! It's Bob's favorite and if I have to watch it one more time!! Well, I'll do it. At least I've got the dip! But I'm kind of sick of that movie Bob! If I have to watch *Braveheart*, then you have to watch *The English Patient*!)

∽ ∽ ∽

Asiago and Artichoke Dip

2 packages (8 ounces) cream cheese, softened

1 cup mayonnaise

2 scallions, finely chopped

2 cloves fresh garlic, minced

1 can (14 ounces) quartered artichoke hearts, drained

1½ cups shredded asiago cheese

1/2 cup sundried tomatoes packed in oil, drained and chopped

Preheat oven to 350 degrees. Spray a small casserole dish with cooking spray. In a large bowl, use a mixer to beat cream cheese, mayonnaise, and garlic until smooth. Stir in artichoke hearts, sundried tomatoes, scallions and cheese. Bake uncovered for 20 to 30 minutes until bubbly and golden. Serve warm with crackers or warm crusty bread.

∾ ∾ ∾

This dip is a great "movie night" treat.   It's really rich and just yummy!! Snuggle up on the couch and enjoy! It's a great make ahead party dip too! Just bake it when you're ready to dive in.

∾ ∾ ∾

Hot Crab Dip

1 package (8 ounces) cream cheese, softened

1 cup mayonnaise

1 teaspoon Worcestershire sauce

2 teaspoons lemon juice

Dash of hot sauce

2 teaspoons Old Bay seafood seasoning

2 scallions, chopped

1 can (4.25 ounces) canned crabmeat, drained

1 cup shredded Cheddar cheese

1 teaspoon dried or 1 tablespoon fresh chopped Italian parsley

1/2 teaspoon paprika

Preheat oven to 350 degrees. Use a mixer and mix together first 6 ingredients until smooth. Fold the crab and scallions into the cream cheese mixture. Spread into a small casserole dish that has been sprayed with cooking spray. Top with shredded cheddar cheese. Next, sprinkle with parsley and paprika. Bake 15 to 30 minutes until hot and bubbly. Serve warm with crackers.

∾ ∾ ∾

A great warm dip for fall or winter get togethers. This is another one of Mimi's recipes. A family favorite! We love this one at the holidays, especially after a long day of skiing!

∾ ∾ ∾

Chili and Cheese Dip

2 packages (8 ounces) cream cheese, softened

2 cans (15 ounces) no bean chili

2 to 3 cups shredded cheddar cheese

1/2 cup finely diced red, green, or yellow peppers (optional)

1/4 cup sliced scallions (optional)

Tortilla Chips

Spread the cream cheese in the bottom of a 9" × 13" pan that has been sprayed with cooking spray. Spoon chill over the top so that it covers the cream cheese. Sprinkle cheese on top of the chili. (We LOVE our cheese in Wisconsin, so I'd go for the 3 cups!) Bake in a preheated 350 degree oven for 15 to 30 minutes until it's bubby. If you want to you can sprinkle the scallions and peppers on top. I like them and they look pretty but you know the kids! They may not eat it with "green stuff" on top!

ᘒ ᘒ ᘒ

This is another one of Mimi's. She always kept a couple cans of chili in the cupboard and cream cheese in the fridge, that way if company stopped by at the last minute (and they always seemed to) she was ready. And, of course you gotta have the cheddar too. But we always have that!! Come, on we're Cheeseheads! For game day I sprinkle the top with yellow and green diced peppers and scallions. Gotta do the green and gold thing! We LOVE our Packers!

ᘒ ᘒ ᘒ

Buffalo Chicken Wing Dip

2 packages (8 ounces) softened cream cheese

2 boneless, skinless chicken breast halves, cooked and shredded

2 cups bleu cheese salad dressing

1 cup hot wing sauce

1½ cups shredded cheddar cheese

1½ cups shredded Monterey Jack cheese

1/2 cup scallions, chopped

Spread cream cheese in bottom of baking dish that's been sprayed with cooking spray. Toss together hot wing sauce with the chicken and spoon on top of the cream cheese, spread the bleu cheese dressing over chicken mixture and top with both shredded cheeses. Bake at 350 degrees for 15 to 25 minutes until cheese is melted and bubbly. Top with scallions. Serve with celery sticks, raw baby carrots or carrot sticks and your favorite crackers or chips.

∽ ∽ ∽

If you like wings, you'll love this dip! It's way easier to make than wings too! Great to serve at all those football parties!

∽ ∽ ∽

Reuben Dip

1/2 cup mayonnaise

1/2 cup sour cream

1 package (8 ounces) cream cheese, softened

3 tablespoons ketchup

2 cups shredded Swiss cheese

1 tablespoon prepared horseradish (optional)

1 cup corned beef, finely chopped

1 cup sauerkraut, drained

Preheat oven to 350 degrees. In a bowl, use a mixer to mix mayonnaise, sour cream, ketchup, and cream cheese until smooth. Stir in remaining ingredients by hand. Spoon mixture into a small casserole dish that has been sprayed with cooking spray. Bake in a preheated 350 degree oven for 20 to 25 minutes. Serve warm out of the oven with cocktail rye bread, bagel chips, or crackers.

∾ ∾ ∾

Got leftover corned beef from St. Paddy's Day? Use it to make this dip. If not, go to the deli and have them slice you up some corned beef. Bottom line – make this dip!!

∾ ∾ ∾

Pizza Dip

1 package (8 ounces) cream cheese, softened

1 cup pizza sauce

1/4 cup onion finely diced

1/4 cup green pepper finely diced

2 cups mozzarella cheese, shredded

1 can (2.25 ounces) sliced black olives

1/4 cup sliced pepperoni, finely diced

Press cream cheese in the bottom of 9-inch glass pie plate or small casserole dish that's been sprayed with cooking spray. Spread pizza sauce over cream cheese and layer remaining ingredients in the order listed. Bake in a preheated 350° oven for 15 to 25 minutes or until hot and bubbly. Serve with warm bread sticks or your favorite crackers.

જી જી જી

My kids love this one minus the veggies. So you can leave them out. No big deal!!

જી જી જી

Wisconsin Bleu Cheesecake

2 containers (8 ounces) mascarpone cheese

1½ cups (12 ounces) crumbled bleu cheese or gorgonzola, divided

3 eggs

1/4 cup sour cream

1/4 cup fig jam or apricot preserves

1 tablespoon fresh rosemary chopped

2 teaspoons flour

Pinch salt

Black pepper, freshly ground

Parchment paper

Aged balsamic vinegar

Preheat oven to 325 degrees. Spray an 8" spring form pan with cooking spray. Line bottom with parchment paper and spray again. In large bowl, use a mixer to beat cream cheese and mascarpone cheese until smooth. Add all but 1/4 cup of bleu cheese, beat until creamy. Add eggs, one at a time, beating well after each addition. Add sour cream, jam, flour, salt and pepper. Beat until combined. Pour into pan. Place a shallow pan of water in the oven on the shelf below the cheesecake. Bake 30 minutes, sprinkle reserved bleu cheese over top and bake for 15 minutes, until lightly browned. Cool to room temperature. Remove cheesecake from pan and cut into wedges. Serve warm with aged balsamic vinegar drizzled on top. Thanks to Chef Chris Mangless, The Traveling Chef, for this one.

Cheese Fondue

1 large clove garlic, peeled and halved

4 cups shredded Gruyere cheese

3 tablespoons flour

1/8 teaspoon white pepper

1 cup dry white wine

1 loaf crusty French bread, cut into 1 inch cubes

Fresh vegetables like grape tomatoes, broccoli and cauliflower florets

Rub the bottom and inside of the fondue pot with the garlic halves to add flavor. In a mixing bowl, combine the shredded cheese, flour and pepper. Mix so the flour coats the cheese and set aside. Heat the fondue pot to medium heat. Add wine, heat until warm; do not boil. Add the cheese, a handful at a time, stirring until the cheese melts and the mixture is a light creamy sauce. Adjust the heat to keep the cheese warm but not too hot. Dip cubes of bread and veggies into the hot cheese.

෩ ෩ ෩

I LOVE fondue. My grandmother Mimi and her husband Homer had a big fondue party during the holidays every year. Now my family does it too. What fun! Come on, do fondue!!

෩ ෩ ෩

Baked Brie in Puff Pastry

1 round wheel (8 ounces) brie cheese

1/2 package (17.5 ounces) frozen puff pastry (one sheet), thawed

2 tablespoons toasted sliced almonds (optional)

1/4 cup apricot preserves or raspberry jam

1 egg, beaten

Foil or parchment paper

Crackers or sliced French bread

Preheat the oven to 425 degrees. Line a piece of foil or parchment paper on a jelly roll pan or cookie sheet. Lay the pastry on the foil or parchment and use a rolling pin to roll it out a bit. Place wheel of brie in the center of the pastry. Spread the preserves or jam on top of the cheese. Place nuts on top, wrap the puff pastry dough around the cheese. Flip it over so the prettiest side is on top. Brush the pastry with the egg. Bake for 20 to 35 minutes until pastry is golden. Let cool a few minutes before serving. Place on a pretty plate surrounded by sliced French bread or crackers.

⌒⌒ ⌒⌒ ⌒⌒

This is one of the recipes that people go crazy over. You end up looking like a rock star! LOVE THAT!! The best part, it's so easy!! Go ahead and have fun with this and change it up a bit. Instead of jam use some cranberry sauce and pecans for the holidays. Or you can skip the jam and nuts and just bake the brie alone. It's all good! Really good!

⌒⌒ ⌒⌒ ⌒⌒

Baked Brie with Apples

2 tablespoons butter

2 apples, peeled, cored and cut in small pieces

1/4 cup brown sugar

Pinch of nutmeg

Pinch of cinnamon

1 round wheel (8 ounces) brie cheese

1/2 package (17.5 ounces) frozen puff pastry (one sheet), thawed

1 egg

1 tablespoon water

1/4 cup toasted pecans (optional)

Crackers or French bread

Extra Sliced apples

In a medium saucepan, melt butter over medium heat. Add the diced apples, sugar, cinnamon and nutmeg, stir well to combine. Cook, stirring occasionally until the apples start to get a little soft. Let cool a bit. Line a baking sheet with parchment paper. Place the puff pastry on the parchment. Using a sharp knife cut the wheel of brie in half. Spread half the apple mixture on top of the bottom half of cheese. Next, sprinkle pecans on top. Then, top with remaining piece of cheese, rind side up. Spoon the remaining apples and nuts on top. Bring the puff pastry up around the edges of the layers. Cut any extra dough and seal it up the bundle. Flip it over so that the pretty side is facing up. In a bowl, beat egg and water together. Brush the surface of the puff pastry lightly with the egg wash. Bake in a preheated 425 degree oven for 25 to 40 minutes, or until golden brown. Let cool a few minutes, then transfer to a serving platter with a knife and crackers or bread and sliced apple.

∾ ∾ ∾

Can you tell I love brie? So does my mom! She taught me good! Anyway, here's a great one for fall or the holidays. You can use some of the extra pastry dough to make leaves or holly on the top. I promise! Just two more brie recipes in this book for you folks who just aren't into it. But, really you should try it!

∾ ∾ ∾

Raspberry Brie Tarts

2 packages (2.1 ounces) of mini phyllo pastry shells (30 shells)

8 ounces Brie cheese

3 to 4 tablespoons raspberry spreadable fruit

Preheat oven to 350 degrees. Place shells on an ungreased jelly roll pan. Cut cheese into tiny cubes. Place a few cheese cubs into each shell. Top each with a little fruit spread. Bake for 4 to 8 minutes. Do not over bake. Serve warm.

❧ ❧ ❧

Okay, it doesn't get much easier than this. These are so cute and elegant too! Line them up on a pretty tray surrounded by a few fresh raspberries and you look like you hired a caterer! Gotta love that!

❧ ❧ ❧

Bacon Wrapped Water Chestnuts

1/2 pound sliced bacon

1 can whole water chestnuts

1/2 cup soy sauce

1/4 to 1/2 cup brown sugar

Plain wooden toothpicks

Place water chestnuts in a small bowl and cover with soy sauce and let them soak for a few minutes. Remove and wrap the water chestnuts with one piece of bacon and secure with toothpicks. Place in baking dish. Top each with brown sugar and pour the soy that is remaining in the bowl over the top. Bake in a preheated 400 degree oven for 15 to 25 minutes or until the bacon gets crisp.

Here's another family favorite. WE LOVE THESE! So much so that we even served them at my wedding reception. We just had too! My sister, Cary, usually gets stuck making them at family get-togethers. They're not hard! They just take a little time to roll up. Thanks Cares! WARNING! If you do make these, make plenty! Just to be safe you may want to double or even triple the recipe. You'll be glad you did! I'm telling you people gobble them right up!

Brat Bundles

1 tube (8 ounces) refrigerated crescent rolls

4 to 5 smoked cheddar bratwurst or smoked regular brats or polish sausages

1 egg, beaten

Separate the dough into four pieces, keeping triangles together, so that you have 4 big squares. Cut each square into one inch strips with a pizza cutter for a total of 32 pieces. Cut the brats into one inch pieces for a total of 32 pieces.

Roll the dough around each piece of bratwurst. Brush with egg wash. Place the bundles upright on a cookie sheet and bake in a preheated 425 degree oven for 12 to 15 minutes until golden. Great with spicy mustard for dipping.

〜 〜 〜

These are good, really good! They're kind of fun to make too! Let the kids help. Make lots! These are going to go over big at your game day get-together!! Thanks to Sarah of Berlin for this one! The crew loved them! When I make them, my kids gobble them right up, Bob too!

〜 〜 〜

Ranch Won Tons

1 pound bulk pork sausage

1 cup shredded sharp cheddar cheese

1 cup Monterey Jack cheese or pepper jack cheese if you want them spicy

3/4 cup prepared ranch dressing

1 can (4.25 ounces) chopped black olives (optional)

1/2 cup finely diced red or green bell pepper, or a little of both

1 package (12 ounces) won ton wrappers

1 to 2 tablespoons vegetable oil

Brush won ton wrappers with vegetable oil and put into cupcake tin to form little cups. Bake in a preheated 350 degree oven until edges just start to turn brown. Cool. Fry sausage and drain. Mix sausage, ranch dressing, olives and cheese together. Put a spoonful of mix into each cup. Bake in a preheated 350 degree oven for 5 to 8 minutes until warmed and cheese is bubbly. Sprinkle with diced peppers when they come out of the oven. Makes about 25 appetizers. Eat warm!

෨ ෨ ෨

These are really fun and different! They take a little time to put together but they're worth it. Try using "hot" sausage if you can take the heat! These make a great game day munchie!

෨ ෨ ෨

Party Meatballs

2 pounds lean ground beef

1 cup fresh bread crumbs (just plain white bread that you throw in the food processor or crumble by hand)

2 eggs, slightly beaten

2 tablespoons minced dried onions

1/2 teaspoon garlic powder

1/4 teaspoon salt

1/4 teaspoon pepper

Sauce:

1 can (15 ounces) jellied cranberry sauce

1 bottle (12 ounces) chili sauce

2 tablespoons brown sugar

1 tablespoon lemon juice

Preheat oven to 350 degrees. In large bowl, combine all meatball ingredients; mix well. Using rounded teaspoonfuls, shape into 1 inch balls. Bake for 20–30 minutes or until browned. In a large pan, heat sauce ingredients stirring constantly until well blended. Put meatballs and sauce in a slow cooker or chafing dish. Heat on low. Serve with toothpicks.

~ ~ ~

A party favorite! You can make the meatballs and sauce a day or two ahead of time and heat them up right before the party. Sometimes I double the recipe just to make sure there's enough. Guys (and gals) LOVE meatballs! They freeze well too!

~ ~ ~

Seafood Stuffed Mushrooms

2 tablespoons butter

2 tablespoons finely diced onion

2 tablespoons finely diced celery

2 tablespoons finely diced red pepper

1 tablespoon dry white wine or chicken stock

1/2 teaspoon garlic salt

2 teaspoons lemon juice

1 can (4.25 ounces) lump crabmeat, drained

6 to 8 pieces of shrimp, cooked and finely diced

I package (8 ounces) softened cream cheese

12 to 16 large stuffing mushrooms

1 cup shredded Swiss cheese

1/2 cup crushed garlic croutons

Clean mushrooms and remove stems. Place mushrooms in a 9" × 13" pan that's been sprayed with cooking spray. Preheat oven to 375 degrees. Melt butter in a skillet over medium heat and sauté onion, celery, and red pepper until soft. Season with garlic salt. Add wine or stock. Cook for another minute. Add crabmeat and shrimp. Add lemon juice and cream cheese and mix well. Spoon a little mixture into mushrooms caps. Sprinkle each mushroom top with some cheese and then some croutons. Bake 15 to 25 minutes until golden.

These are Bob's absolute favorite! He's a big "mushroom guy!" They are great to serve at a dinner party because you can make them ahead and just bake them when everyone gets there. Sometimes I'll make them just for us! A great start to a date night or movie night at home! Hey, when's the last time you did that? Maybe it's time!

Crab Bites

1 can (4.75 ounces) crabmeat, drained well

2 tablespoons finely diced red pepper

4 tablespoons butter, softened

1 jar (4 ounces) Old English cheese

1/2 teaspoon garlic salt

2 tablespoons mayonnaise

Dash of Worcestershire sauce

6 English muffins, split

1 tablespoon finely chopped scallions or Italian parsley for garnish

Mix together the first six ingredients. Cut each English muffin like a pizza into 8 bite-sized pieces. Spread some of the crab mixture on each piece. Bake on a cookie sheet in a preheated 375 degree oven for 10 to 15 minutes. Serve right away! Garnish with scallions or parsley before serving.

∾ ∾ ∾

These get gobbled right up away so you might want to double the recipe if company is coming. They go over big at parties too! Go ahead and slice your muffins up and make the crab spread ahead of time. Then you can throw them in the oven just before you want to serve them. Now, get out there and enjoy the party!

∾ ∾ ∾

Amazing Cheese Bread

1 cup shredded asiago cheese

1 cup shredded parmesan cheese

1/2 cup grated romano cheese, divided

1½ cups mayonnaise

2 fresh garlic cloves, minced

1/2 teaspoon dried oregano

1 loaf focaccia bread or crusty French bread

3 tablespoons chopped Italian parsley

Warm marinara sauce (optional)

In a medium size bowl mix together mayonnaise with the garlic, oregano, parsley, parmesan, asiago, and 1/4 cup of the romano cheese. Slice bread loaf in half lengthwise. Spread the cheese mixture on each half of the bread. Sprinkle the tops with the rest of the romano cheese. Place bread on a cookie sheet and bake in a preheated 425 degree oven for 8 to 12 minutes or until the top is golden brown. You can also broil the bread for a minute or two to get the top a little browned. But if you do decide to broil it, stay right there and watch it! I'm always burning the bread. (HATE THAT!) Cut into strips and serve. If you want you can serve this with marinara sauce for dipping.

ϡ ϡ ϡ

This is a winner!! It goes great with some of my pasta and casserole recipes. This bread is so good that they serve it over at Lambeau Field on game day. Thanks to Chef Leo, who's in charge of the food over there, for giving me the recipe. I've been making it for my family ever since! Make it for yours!!

ϡ ϡ ϡ

Bob's Favorite Ranch Snack Mix

8 cups of assorted square cereal (corn, rice, bran and wheat)

1½ cups of peanuts (optional)

2 cups small pretzels

2 cups of miniature bagel chips

2 cups sesame snack stix

1¼ cups of butter

3 tablespoons Worcestershire sauce

1 packet (1 ounce) dry ranch dressing mix

Melt butter, Worcestershire sauce and ranch dressing mix. Pour remaining ingredients into a big bowl. Pour in butter mixture. Toss until the cereal mixture is evenly coated. Spread onto a big cookie sheet or jelly roll pan. Bake in a preheated 250 degree oven for about 30 minutes. Don›t over bake! Store the mix in an airtight container. Keeps for up to 3 weeks but it won't last that long. Trust me!

❧ ❧ ❧

Bob loves any kind of snack mix. He's in his car driving to different courthouses all the time and if there's no time for lunch, a handful or two of this will get him through 'til dinner. Every Christmas my sister, Cary, sends him a big container of homemade snack mix. Then, I get "the business" about how I never make it for him. Okay, okay, I'll try to make it more often.

❧ ❧ ❧

Seasoned Pretzels

2 bags (16 ounces) small pretzels

1 packet (1 ounce) dry ranch salad dressing mix

3/4 cup canola or vegetable oil

1½ teaspoons dill weed

1½ teaspoons garlic powder

Place pretzels in a large bowl. Combine remaining ingredients and pour over pretzels. Stir to coat. Pour into a large baking pan. Bake at 200° for 45 minutes to an hour, stirring every 15 minutes. Store in an airtight container for up to 3 weeks. I put them in a bunch of snack bags. Need snacks? I got 'em.

∽ ∽ ∽

Talk about a great way to take a boring, cheap bag of pretzels to the next level. These rock! My kids (and Bob) love 'em. Great with the beer dip recipe earlier in this chapter, or as an after school snack. I also pack them in the kids' lunches.

∽ ∽ ∽

SUPER GOOD SALADS

Raspberry Vinaigrette

3/4 cup raspberries, fresh or frozen

1/4 cup sugar

1/4 cup cider vinegar

3/4 cup canola oil

Salt and pepper to taste

In a sauce pan, heat the raspberries with the sugar and cook until sugar is dissolved. Let it cool a bit. Put the mixture in a blender and blend raspberries with vinegar. While blender is running, slowly add oil. Season with a little salt and pepper. Keeps up to a week in fridge.

∽ ∽ ∽

This dressing is so pretty! I love the color! It's also so quick and easy! There's nothing like homemade salad dressing!! I like to toss this with some spring mix lettuce, toasted walnuts, and some crumbled bleu cheese. Wow, now that's a good salad!

∽ ∽ ∽

Nice and Light Vinaigrette

1/3 cup white balsamic vinegar

1 cup light olive oil or canola oil

1/2 teaspoon salt

2 teaspoons sugar

1/4 teaspoon fresh ground black pepper

1 teaspoon Italian seasoning

1 clove garlic, minced

Shake up all the ingredients in a glass jar with a screw-on lid. Refrigerate and shake well before serving. Keeps up to a week in the fridge.

∾ ∾ ∾

I got this recipe from my Aunt Bridgett. She's actually more like a sister because she's only about 5 years older than me, but I love to call her Aunt because it bugs her! Luv ya Bridge! Anyway, she's always in charge of making the salads at our family get-togethers. This dressing works on just about any salad but we like it tossed with chopped romaine, sliced cucumbers, a little diced celery, red pepper, toasted walnuts and crumbled bleu cheese.

∾ ∾ ∾

Italian Vinaigrette

1/2 cup red wine vinegar

1½ cups canola, vegetable, or olive oil

1 to 2 cloves garlic, minced or crushed

1 teaspoon sugar

1/2 teaspoon salt

1/4 teaspoon black pepper

1 teaspoon Dijon mustard

1 teaspoon Italian seasoning

Shake it all up in a glass jar with a screw-on lid. Refrigerate until ready to use. Shake well before serving. Keeps in the fridge for a week or so.

෩ ෩ ෩

This is my go-to dressing when I need a quick salad to go with pasta or pizza. Toss it with some lettuce, cukes, and tomatoes and you're set! Maybe some fresh grated parmesan cheese and croutons on top too! (My recipe for home made croutons is coming up later in this chapter. It's really easy and they're way better than the boxed ones!)

෩ ෩ ෩

Greek Vinaigrette

1/4 cup white wine vinegar

1/4 cup lemon juice

1 tablespoon oregano

2 cloves garlic minced or crushed

1/4 teaspoon salt

1/4 teaspoon pepper

1½ cups olive oil

Shake it all up in a glass jar with a screw-on lid. Refrigerate until ready to use. Shake well before serving. Keeps in the fridge for about a week, maybe even a little longer.

ରେ ରେ ରେ

I love a good Greek salad! Just toss a little of this dressing with chopped romaine, cukes, lettuce, tomatoes, crumbled feta cheese and maybe some artichoke hearts and kalamata olives and I'm lovin' life. Love this with my "Greek Chicken", "Greek Ribeyes", and "Pork Souvlaki" recipes all in the "What's for Dinner? I'm Hungry!" chapter. Can you tell we like Greek food?

ରେ ରେ ରେ

"The Best" Bleu Cheese Dressing

1 cup bleu cheese, crumbled

1 cup mayonnaise

1 cup sour cream

3 tablespoons of milk

2 teaspoons lemon juice

1 teaspoon hot sauce

2 teaspoons Worcestershire sauce

1/2 teaspoon celery salt

1 teaspoon ground mustard

1 teaspoon onion powder

2 teaspoons garlic powder

1 teaspoon sugar

Salt and pepper to taste

Combine first 12 ingredients and mix well. Season with a little salt and pepper. Refrigerate for at least 2 hours before serving. If it's too thick, thin it out with a little milk. Keeps in the fridge for a week.

I love bleu cheese dressing. I think this one is "The Best" I have ever tasted. Thanks to Chef Abbey for this one! Serve it on any greens, or even better, on the wedge salad on the next page.

Wedge Salad

1 head of iceberg lettuce

8 slices of vine ripe tomatoes

Salt and pepper

8 pieces of crispy bacon, crumbled

1/2 cup fresh bleu cheese, crumbled

Bleu cheese dressing

Remove core from lettuce. Cut lettuce into 4 wedges. Place one lettuce wedge on each plate. Place 2 slices of tomatoes next to each wedge. Season the tomatoes with a little salt and pepper. Top the wedge with bleu cheese dressing, some crumbled bleu cheese, and bacon. Serve with fresh ground black pepper on the top.

෬ ෬ ෬

I'm not a huge fan of iceberg lettuce but you've just gotta use it in this recipe! It's so good with those beautiful beef steak tomatoes in the summer. Serve this with a big juicy grilled steak and a baked potato and I'm lovin' life!

෬ ෬ ෬

Hearts of Romaine Caesar Salad

3/4 cup olive oil

1 to 2 cloves garlic, minced

1/2 teaspoon freshly ground pepper

1 teaspoon Dijon mustard

1 teaspoon anchovy paste (comes in a tube, if you don't have it, no big deal)

2 tablespoons fresh lemon juice

1 tablespoon red wine vinegar

1 teaspoon of Worcestershire sauce

2 tablespoons mayonnaise

2 tablespoons grated Parmesan cheese

Hearts of romaine lettuce

Shredded parmesan cheese

Garlic croutons

Whisk together lemon juice, garlic, mustard, mayonnaise, Worcestershire, anchovy paste, salt and pepper. Slowly whisk in olive oil. Stir in grated parmesan. You can also throw all the dressing ingredients in the blender and blend until smooth. Refrigerate dressing until ready to use. If it gets a little too thick just stir in some water. Dip whole romaine leaves into dressing. Place 4 to 6 leaves on a plate. Top with shredded parmesan cheese and more fresh black pepper. Serve with garlic croutons. I make my own, but you don't have to. If you want to give it a try, the recipe is on the next page. It's easy! Promise!!

$$\backsim \quad \backsim \quad \backsim$$

When we go out for dinner and a choice of salad is offered, Bob always goes for the Caesar. It is his favorite. We've all had that Caesar salad that could have been better!! (You know what I'm talking about!) That's why you gotta try this one! I love using whole romaine lettuce leaves because they look so pretty, especially on date night at home or when company is coming, but you can use chopped romaine too. Notice, no raw eggs in this dressing either for folks worried about that.

$$\backsim \quad \backsim \quad \backsim$$

Homemade Croutons

1 loaf day old French bread, cut in cubes

1/4 to 1/2 cup olive oil or melted butter (Just depends on how much bread)

1 tablespoon dried parsley

2 to 3 teaspoons dried Italian seasoning

2 to 3 teaspoons garlic powder

A little salt and pepper

1/4 cup grated parmesan cheese (optional)

Preheat oven to 300 degrees. Place all ingredients in a bowl and toss well. Spread out in one layer on a cookie sheet or jelly roll pan (you might need two pans). Bake for 12 to 25 minutes until golden. Be careful not to burn them! (Seems like I always do!)

~ ~ ~

Ever tried making your own croutons? It is so darn easy you can't believe it! And, the house smells so good when you do it! Every time I do it the kids come running downstairs, and ask what I am making. Seems like a lot of the croutons end up in their mouths right then and there instead of in my salads. Oh well, there could be worse snacks! Anyway you'll never go back to the boxed kind once you start making your own. It's a great way to use up leftover French bread, or any kind of firm, crusty bread!

~ ~ ~

Strawberry Spinach Salad

Dressing:

1/3 cup white wine vinegar

1 teaspoon salt

1/2 cup sugar

1 teaspoon dry mustard

1½ tablespoons fresh red onion, minced

1 cup vegetable oil

1½ tablespoons poppy seeds

Shake together in a jar and refrigerate. Keeps in the fridge for one week.

Salad:

2 cups fresh strawberries, sliced

1 big bag (9 ounces) fresh spinach

1 cup whole pecans

2 tablespoons butter

Place butter in a skillet. Toast pecans in butter for a couple minutes on medium heat. Be careful! Do not burn the nuts! I always seem to burn the nuts! (HATE THAT!!) Let the nuts cool a bit. When ready to serve, toss spinach, strawberries and pecans together in a big bowl. Drizzle with some, not all, the dressing. The extra dressing keeps in the fridge for about a week.

∾ ∾ ∾

This is by far my favorite summer salad. It won first prize in a summer recipe contest I had on my show. It's fresh, pretty, fun and easy. Serve grilled chicken on the top and you've got a delicious, light lunch or dinner. Love those buttery pecans!! Thanks Harriet!

∾ ∾ ∾

Pear and Walnut Salad

1/2 cup olive oil

3 tablespoons walnut oil

1/4 balsamic vinegar

Salt and pepper

8 to 10 cups spring mix lettuce

1/4 cup red onion, thinly sliced

1/2 cup crumbled gorgonzola or bleu cheese

2 sliced pears

1/2 cup toasted walnuts

Whisk or shake the first 3 ingredients together. Season with a little salt and pepper. Toss some of the dressing with the lettuce. (You may not need to use all the dressing). Place lettuce on 4 to 6 plates or on one big platter. Top with onions, pears, nuts, and cheese. Extra dressing keeps in the fridge for at least a couple weeks.

∽ ∽ ∽

This is the easiest salad to make and everybody goes crazy over. It real simple, pretty, and really good! Make it! Nice in the fall or when you can get pretty red pears, but I like it all year round!

∽ ∽ ∽

Apple Cranberry Salad

1 cup mayonnaise

2 tablespoons apple cider vinegar

2 tablespoons apple cider

1/2 cup brown sugar

8 to 10 cups spring mix lettuce

1 diced green apple with skin on

1 diced red apple with skin on

1/4 cup dried cranberries

1/4 cup chopped pecans, toasted

Whisk together the first four ingredients until smooth. Cover and refrigerate for a few hours. You can make this dressing up to 2 days ahead. Just stir well before serving and if it's too thick, add a little more apple cider. Divide lettuce up on 4 to 6 plates. Drizzle a little dressing on top of each salad. Top with apples, cranberries and nuts.

∽ ∽ ∽

This salad is really nice in the fall. I serve it at Thanksgiving. It's also wonderful at holiday get-togethers because it's so pretty! To toast nuts, place them in a dry skillet and cook them on medium heat for a few minutes. Be careful not to burn them- I almost always do! It's a running joke , "Mom burned the nuts again!!" Try to get that smell out of the house! So, why do you toast the nuts? They just taste better, that's all. But you don't have to!

∽ ∽ ∽

Mimi's Layered Salad

2 cups mayonnaise

2 cups sour cream

2/3 cup parmesan cheese

1/2 teaspoon black pepper

1/2 teaspoon garlic salt

1 to 2 heads iceberg lettuce, cores removed

2 cups celery, finely diced

2 cups frozen peas

1 can sliced water chestnuts, drained

1/2 pound bacon, cooked and crumbled

4 hard boiled eggs, chopped

2 cups shredded cheddar cheese

1/4 cup chopped scallions

In a bowl mix first 5 ingredients together until smooth. In a 9" × 13" glass pan or big pretty clear glass bowl layer large chunks lettuce, then celery, peas, water chestnuts, bacon, and eggs. Then carefully spread mayonnaise dressing on top. Sprinkle cheddar cheese and scallions on top. Cover with plastic wrap and chill. Cut into squares when ready to serve. This salad can be made several hours before serving. It is best if it's served the day you make it.

∽ ∽ ∽

Mimi was known for this salad. It's still one of my favorites. The best part is you can make the entire salad ahead of time, and because the dressing is on top, the salad doesn't get mushy. Thanks Mimi. I think of you every time I make it!

∽ ∽ ∽

Layered Taco Salad

3 cups sour cream

1 cup mayonnaise

1 teaspoon chili powder

1 teaspoon garlic salt

Few dashes hot sauce

1½ pounds lean ground beef

1 package taco seasoning

1 to 2 heads of iceberg lettuce, cores removed

1 cup corn

1 can (15 ounces) kidney or black beans, drained and rinsed

3 scallions, chopped

2 to 3 cups shredded Mexican blended cheese

1 medium tomato chopped

1 can (2.5 ounces) sliced black olives

Tortilla chips

Salsa

In a bowl, whisk together first five ingredients. Cover and refrigerate until ready to use. Brown the beef in a skillet. Add taco seasoning and some water according to package instructions. Let cool. In a large clear glass bowl or clear 9" × 13" glass pan, start layering. First cut lettuce into big chunks and put in the bowl or pan. Next spread cooled taco meat, then beans and corn over the lettuce. Carefully spread the sour cream mixture on top like you frost a cake. Sprinkle cheese, tomatoes, olives, and scallions on top. Cover with plastic wrap and refrigerate until ready to serve. Serve with tortilla chips and salsa.

〜 〜 〜

I came up with this one. It's a lot like Mimi's layered salad but if you like tacos you'll love this! You can totally make this a few hours ahead. It's great for potlucks. We LOVE our potlucks in Wisconsin!! It also makes a nice light dinner.

〜 〜 〜

Layered Italian Salad

For the dressing:

1/2 cup mayonnaise

1/3 cup white vinegar

1 teaspoon vegetable oil

2 tablespoons corn syrup

2 tablespoons grated parmesan cheese

2 tablespoons grated romano cheese

1 clove of garlic, minced or pressed

Pinch salt

1/2 teaspoon of dried Italian seasoning

1/2 teaspoon parsley flakes

1 tablespoon fresh lemon juice

Put all ingredients in a jar and shake it up. Refrigerate until ready to serve. Shake well before serving. Keeps in the fridge for up to a week.

For the Salad:

1 to 2 heads romaine or iceberg lettuce, chopped

Half of a red onion, sliced thin

1½ cups black olives, cut in half

1/2 cup sliced pepperoncini

1 ½ cups grape or cherry tomatoes

1 ½ cups croutons

1/2 cup shredded parmesan cheese

Layer salad in that order and pour on dressing before serving. Top with croutons and parmesan.

Country Club Salad

For the Maple Mustard Dressing:

4 tablespoons maple syrup

1/4 cup apple cider vinegar

3 tablespoons Dijon mustard

1 tablespoon chopped shallots

3/4 cup canola oil

Salt and pepper

Whisk first five ingredients together. Season with a little salt and pepper. Extra dressing can be stored in the fridge for up to a week.

For the Salad:

1 head Romaine lettuce, chopped

6 to 10 cups spring mix lettuce

2 medium tomatoes, seeded and finely chopped

2 cooked chicken breasts, diced

6 strips bacon, cooked and crumbled

1 avocado, diced

2 tablespoons, finely diced red onion

1 cup bleu cheese, crumbled

6 ounces bow tie pasta, boiled and cooled

Toss together all ingredients in a large bowl. Before serving, toss with some but not all of the dressing. Serve salad on a large platter or on individual plates.

BBQ Chicken Salad

2 to 3 skinless, boneless chicken breast halves

1 head romaine lettuce, chopped

6 to 8 cups spring mix lettuce

1 cup tomatoes, seeded and diced

1 diced ripe avocado

1 cup corn (fresh off the cob if it's in season)

1 can (15 ounces) black beans, drained and rinsed

1 cup shredded cheddar cheese

1/2 cup shredded monterey jack cheese

1/4 cup chopped fresh cilantro

2 cups prepared ranch dressing

1 cup BBQ sauce, divided

Grill chicken breasts, brushing with 3/4 of a cup of BBQ sauce. Mix remaining 1/4 cup BBQ sauce with ranch dressing. Chill dressing until ready to serve. Cut grilled chicken into thin strips or chunks. Place lettuce on a large platter or individual plates. Top lettuce with tomatoes, avocados, corn and beans. Next place chicken on top, then cheeses and cilantro. Serve right away with dressing on the side.

Apple Slaw

1 medium cabbage, shredded or a 1 pound bag coleslaw mix

2 apples, cored and diced

1 cup mayonnaise

3 tablespoons apple cider vinegar

1/4 to 1/2 cup toasted pecans (optional)

1/4 cup sugar

3 tablespoons red onion, finely diced

3 tablespoons chopped Italian parsley

Salt and pepper to taste

In a big bowl, whisk together the sugar and vinegar. Next, whisk in the mayonnaise and a little salt and pepper. Toss in the remaining ingredients. Refrigerate for at least a few hours before serving.

 ෬ ෬ ෬

Here's a fun coleslaw recipe. Just something a little different than the usual stuff. Thanks to a long time friend, Chef Ken, for helping me out with this one! Goes over great at all those backyard BBQ's! It's also a nice side with my BBQ beef and BBQ pork sandwich recipes in the "Just throw it in the Slow Cooker" chapter.

 ෬ ෬ ෬

Bacon and Bleu Slaw

3/4 cup mayonnaise

2 tablespoon red wine vinegar

1 tablespoon honey

1 teaspoon celery salt

2 teaspoons Dijon mustard

Salt and pepper

1 medium cabbage shredded or a 1 pound bag coleslaw mix

3 tablespoon chopped Italian parsley

2 tablespoons red onion, finely diced

Half pound of bacon, cooked and crumbled

8 ounces crumbled bleu or gorgonzola cheese

In a big bowl whisk together the first 5 ingredients. Season with a little salt and pepper. Toss in remaining ingredients. Refrigerate at least a few hours before serving.

✿ ✿ ✿

Okay, so you had me at bacon! Talk about a really good slaw! This is it! Great at all those BBQ's and picnics. They'll be asking for this recipe for sure!! Don't like bleu cheese, too bad! (Just kidding!) You can leave it out. Hey, you've still got the bacon in there! Just don't leave that out!

✿ ✿ ✿

Crunchy Asian Slaw

1 to 2 heads Napa cabbage (just depends how big they are)

1/4 cup scallions, chopped

1/4 cup rice wine vinegar

2/3 cup vegetable oil

2 tablespoons sugar

1 tablespoon soy sauce

1 teaspoon sesame oil

1 package (3 ounces) ramen noodles

2 tablespoons sesame seeds

1 cup cashews or slivered almonds (optional)

3 tablespoons butter, melted

1 can (11 ounces) mandarin oranges, drained

Combine vinegar, oil, sugar, soy sauce, seasoning packet from ramen and sesame oil in a jar. Screw on tight and shake until sugar is dissolved. Refrigerate until ready to serve. Preheat oven to 300 degrees. Break the ramen noodles into small pieces. Spread the noodles, nuts, and sesame seeds out on a baking sheet and drizzle with butter. Bake 5 to 10 minutes, until nicely toasted. Be careful not to burn them! Let cool, and place in an airtight container or re-sealable bag until ready to use. When ready to serve, chop cabbage. Toss cabbage and scallions with ramen mixture, oranges and some of the dressing. Serve right away. You may not use all the dressing. Extra dressing can be kept in fridge for up to a week.

My Family's Favorite Baby Red Potato Salad

3 pounds baby red potatoes, washed well and cut into quarters

1 teaspoon salt

1 cup sour cream

2 cups mayonnaise

1 teaspoon garlic salt

1/2 teaspoon black pepper

4 stalks celery, finely diced

4 hard boiled eggs, chopped

4 scallions, chopped

1/4 cup fresh chopped dill

Half pound bacon, cooked and crumbled

Fill a large pan with water. Add potatoes and salt. Bring to a boil over medium high heat. Cook 10 to 20 minutes or until potatoes start to get tender. Don't overcook them- we're not making mashed potatoes! In a large bowl, whisk together next 4 ingredients. Add potatoes and remaining ingredients. Toss to coat. If mixture looks dry, add more mayonnaise. Cover and chill for a few hours or overnight until ready to serve. Before serving, check to see if more mayonnaise is needed. It should be nice and creamy! Garnish with more fresh chopped dill and scallions if you want.

∽ ∽ ∽

People go nuts over this potato salad. It really is out of this world, if I do say so myself! I make it all the time in the summer. We serve it with BBQ chicken or ribs. That's what Bob wants for his birthday dinner every year, BBQ chicken and my potato salad, and maybe an apple pie for dessert. No, I don't make the pie, that's what bakeries are for!!

∽ ∽ ∽

Broccoli Cauliflower Salad

1½ cups mayonnaise

1/3 cup sugar

1/4 cup white vinegar

1/2 cup red onions, finely diced

1 pound bacon, cooked, drained well & crumbled

1 head broccoli

1 head cauliflower

1/2 cup sunflower seeds

1 cup shredded cheese

Mix together mayonnaise, sugar and vinegar. Chop the florets from broccoli and cauliflower into bite sized pieces. Mix in remaining ingredients and add mayonnaise mixture. Refrigerate for 2 hours, or more, before serving.

ꧏ ꧏ ꧏ

Bob loves broccoli. I'm not the biggest fan but I do love this salad. Must be the bacon and sunflower seeds. (Everything is better with a little bacon, right?) This is a great salad to serve at all those summer cookouts!

ꧏ ꧏ ꧏ

Fresh Spinach and Pasta Salad

1 box (16 ounces) penne or bow tie pasta, cooked al dente

7 ounces Bucconcini or Ciliegine (the bite size fresh mozzarella cheese balls), drained

2 cups baby spinach

1 cup pitted kalamata olives, cut in half

1/2 cup grated parmesan cheese

1/2 cup shredded fresh parmesan cheese

3 tablespoons red wine vinegar

Salt and pepper

1/2 cup olive oil

1/4 cup toasted pine nuts

In a large bowl, whisk together red wine vinegar and oil. Season with a little salt and pepper. Toss in pasta, grated parmesan cheese, spinach, olives, pine nuts and mozzarella cheese balls. Toss to coat. Before serving sprinkle shredded parmesan cheese on top. Best if made an hour before serving. If you are going to make it more than an hour ahead of time, cover and refrigerate until ready to serve. I would probably toss it with a little more olive oil before serving.

∾ ∾ ∾

I LOVE pine nuts! This pasta salad is great for lunch or even for a light dinner, maybe with some grilled chicken. I like to pack it in a container and take it to the beach, something different than my usual Gurney's sandwich. If you've ever been to Harbor Springs, Michigan, you know what I'm talking about. The best sandwich ever!

∾ ∾ ∾

Tuna Noodle Salad

2 cans (5 ounces) albacore tuna, drained well

1 box (16 ounces) medium shell pasta, cooked and drained

1½ cups celery, finely diced

1 cup frozen peas, thawed

1/4 cup fresh chopped dill

2 to 3 cups mayonnaise

Salt and pepper

In a large bowl, mix together first 5 ingredients. Stir in 2 cups mayonnaise. If mixture seems too dry, add more mayonnaise. Season with salt and pepper to taste. Chill at least an hour before serving. After chilling, check to see if salad needs more mayonnaise.

∽ ∽ ∽

We eat this a lot in the summer. I make it on Sundays and Bob can pack it for lunch during the week. That way he stays away from the two fast food restaurants right next to his office. Or, at least I hope so.

∽ ∽ ∽

My Favorite Chicken Salad

4 chicken breasts, cooked and diced into bite sized pieces (I use a food processor to chop the chicken up finely)

1/4 cup sour cream

1¼ cups mayonnaise

1 tablespoon fresh lemon juice

1/2 teaspoon garlic salt

1/4 teaspoon black pepper

1 to 2 tablespoons dried tarragon (depends how much you like tarragon – I love it!)

1½ cups celery, finely diced

1½ cups red seedless grapes, cut in half

Whisk together sour cream, mayonnaise, tarragon, salt and pepper in a large bowl. Add celery, grapes and chicken and stir to coat. If mixture is too dry add a little more mayonnaise. Refrigerate at least an hour before serving. Taste to see if more salt and pepper is needed. Great served on croissants or in a half melon.

෮ ෮ ෮

Gotta have chicken salad in the summer, right? I've been making this one for years!! It's still my favorite! Simple and fresh! Give "My Secret Way to Bake Chicken Breasts" at the beginning of the book a try. I think it's the best way to cook the chicken for this salad and a lot of my other recipes that call for diced or shredded chicken. Just tryin' to make it easy for ya, that's all.

෮ ෮ ෮

Sideline Shrimp Salad

3 pounds shrimp, cooked, peeled and deveined

3 hard boiled eggs, chopped

4 celery stalks, finely chopped

3 scallions, chopped

1 tablespoon dried parsley

1 tablespoon olive oil

2 to 3 teaspoons Cajun seasoning (just depends how spicy you want it)

2 cups mayonnaise

Leaf lettuce to line serving bowl

Tomato wedges

Chop shrimp into bite size pieces. Combine remaining ingredients, except lettuce & tomatoes, and mix well. If too dry add more mayo. Refrigerate at least 1 hour before serving. Place in a lettuce lined serving bowl with tomato wedges. Serve with Club crackers.

෩ ෩ ෩

You won't believe where I got this recipe! It's former Packers' quarterback Brett Favre's favorite. His mom and sister came on the show to make it for me years ago. I tweaked it a bit. It's so good!!

෩ ෩ ෩

Seafood Salad

Dill Dressing:

3/4 cup mayonnaise

1/4 cup sour cream

1 tablespoon lemon juice

3 tablespoons fresh dill or 1 teaspoon dried dill weed

2 teaspoons Old Bay seafood seasoning

Salt and pepper to taste

Salad:

1½ pounds cooked shrimp, peeled and deveined

1 can (4.25 ounces) crab meat

1/4 cup scallion, finely diced

1½ cups finely diced celery

Whisk together dill dressing, toss with remaining ingredients. Cover and refrigerate at least 1 hour. It should be creamy. If it seems a little dry, add more mayonnaise. Great on croissants or crusty French bread.

෨ ෨ ෨

A nice change from chicken salad in the summer! The fresh dill makes this! Add more if you like dill. I LOVE IT!!

෨ ෨ ෨

Door County Cherry Chicken Salad

6 chicken breasts, cooked and shredded or diced

1 cup dried cherries

1½ cups celery, finely diced

2 tablespoons red onion, finely diced

1/2 cup chopped pecans, toasted (optional)

2 to 3 cups mayonnaise

1 tablespoon fresh lemon juice

1/2 teaspoon black pepper

1/2 teaspoon garlic salt

In a large bowl, whisk together 2 cups mayonnaise, lemon juice, garlic salt, and peper. Toss in remaining ingredients. If mixture seems a little dry, add more mayonnaise. Add more salt and pepper if needed. Chill for 2 to 4 hours before serving. Great on croissants or in flour tortilla wraps.

༄ ༄ ༄

Here's another great chicken salad recipe. I make this one at the cottage a lot. Reminds me of summer in Door County. We grow a lot of wonderful cherries up there! Have you ever been to Door County? If not, you gotta go!! Just beautiful, and nice people too! Make sure to stop at one of the farm markets to pick up some cherries!

༄ ༄ ༄

Candy Apple Salad

8 to 10 crunchy apples, cored and chopped (no need to peel them)

6 snickers candy bars, chopped (it's a little easier to chop them when they are cold, so throw them in the freezer for a minute)

2 cups dried cherries

1 container (16 ounces) frozen whipped topping, thawed

1 cup sour cream

1/4 cup toasted pecans or walnuts (optional)

In a big bowl, combine whipped topping and sour cream. Add the apples, candy bars, and cherries. Mix together and place nuts on top if you want.

∾ ∾ ∾

I thought I'd end this chapter with this salad. Actually, I'm not sure if this is a salad or a dessert. Let's call it a salad! I feel better eating it that way. Thanks to the folks at Seaquest Orchard in Door County for this one. They grow bunches of apples and cherries. It's a fun place to take the family in summer or fall! I understand this is a recipe the family has been making for years. Thanks for sharin' the love!

∾ ∾ ∾

SOUP'S ON

We're Talkin' Seriously Good Soup!

Tomato Basil Bisque

2 cans (28 ounces) diced fire roasted tomatoes

3½ cups heavy cream

1/4 cup dried basil

1 cup shredded parmesan or mozzarella cheese

3 tablespoons sugar

Salt and pepper

Extra grated or shredded parmesan cheese

Chopped fresh basil

In a large soup pan stir in the cream, sugar, tomatoes with juice, and a little salt and pepper together and bring to a boil. Simmer for a minute or two. Turn down heat and blend the soup with an immersion blender until it's pretty smooth. If you don't have an immersion blender, let the tomatoes and cream mixture cool a bit and blend it with your regular blender in batches, return soup to the pot. Bring the soup back to a simmer. Now, whisk in the basil and cheese. Taste to see if a little more salt and pepper is needed. Serve in bowls with extra cheese and chopped fresh basil on top.

∾ ∾ ∾

This soup makes everything all better! Serve this with garlic bread or, better yet, a grilled cheese sandwich for dunking and let me tell you, life is good! If you can't find fired roasted tomatoes, regular canned tomatoes will work fine too. Thanks to Chef Ryan for this one! IT'S AMAZING!!

∾ ∾ ∾

Chicken Pot Pie Soup

6 tablespoons of butter

5 tablespoons of flour

1 cup onions, finely chopped

1 cup celery, finely chopped

Salt and pepper

6 to 8 cups milk

2 to 4 tablespoons chicken soup base

2 cups frozen southern style cubed hash brown potatoes or cooked cubed potatoes

2 cups mixed frozen vegetables (carrots, green beans, corn, peas)

2 cups diced or shredded cooked chicken

1 cup heavy cream

Fresh chopped Italian parsley

Frozen puff pastry sheets, thawed (optional)

1 egg, beaten (optional)

Oven safe crocks (optional)

In a large soup pan melt butter. Cook onion and celery in butter on medium heat until soft. Season with a little salt and pepper. Add flour and cook on low for a minute, whisking constantly. Add 6 cups of milk and 2 tablespoons of chicken base. Whisk often until it comes to a boil and has thickened. Turn down heat to a low simmer. Add the chicken, potatoes, and vegetables. Let simmer for another 5 minutes. Add the heavy cream. If soup is still too thick, add a little more milk. Taste to see if more chicken soup base or salt and pepper is needed. Serve with fresh chopped parsley on top. To make the crust on top, preheat the oven to 425 degrees. Keep the pastry sheets in the fridge until just before ready to use! Use a rolling pin to quickly roll out the puff pastry sheets a bit. Cut pastry into squares big enough to cover the top of your crocks. Ladle warm soup into oven-safe crocks. Don't fill crocks all the way to the top. Top crocks with pieces of puff pastry. Brush pastry tops with a little of the beaten egg. Bake crocks on a cookie sheet for 12 to 20 minutes until pastry or crust is golden. Sprinkle with chopped parsley.

∽ ∽ ∽

This is the very first recipe I made on my show. People still ask me for it all the time. It's like a big, warm hug in a bowl. You don't have to do the puff pastry on top, but it's so good and looks so cool! So give it a try, it's not that hard to do!! If you're going to skip it (I don't blame you) just serve the soup with warm bread so you can sop up every last bit!

∽ ∽ ∽

Super Quick Homemade Chicken Noodle Soup

3 to 4 tablespoons butter or olive oil

1 medium onion, diced

2 large carrots, diced

4 large stalks celery, diced

2 teaspoons garlic salt

1 teaspoon black pepper

8 to 10 cups chicken stock

3 to 4 chicken breasts, cooked and shredded

1 bag (16 ounces) egg noodles (we like the Amish noodles)

4 tablespoons chopped fresh Italian parsley, or 2 tablespoons dried

In a large soup pan, melt butter. Cook onions, carrots and celery in the butter for about 5 minutes until they start to get soft. Season with garlic salt and pepper. Add chicken and 8 cups of stock. Simmer for a few minutes. Add parsley and cooked noodles just before serving. I don't like to add the noodles 'til the very end, that way they don't get mushy. If you like more broth, add more chicken stock.

∾ ∾ ∾

My mom is known for her homemade chicken noodle soup. When she makes it, it's an all day thing. I don't have all day, so here's how I make it. When the kids have colds, this soup really does seem to help. I have a secret way to bake chicken for soups and casseroles! Check it out at the very beginning of the book. It's a real time saver!

∾ ∾ ∾

Chicken Wild Rice Soup

1 box (6 ounces) long grain and wild rice mix, prepared according to pkg. directions

1 to 2 cups cooked chicken shredded or diced

6 tablespoons of butter

1 cup onions, finely diced

1 cup carrots, finely diced

1 cup celery, finely diced

Salt and pepper

5 tablespoons flour

6 to 7 cups milk

2 to 3 tablespoons chicken soup base

1 cup frozen corn or canned corn

1/4 cup heavy cream

Chopped Italian parsley

Toasted sliced almonds

In a large soup pan, cook the onions, carrots and celery in butter for a few minutes until they start to get soft. Season with a little salt and pepper. Stir in flour and cook a minute or two, whisking constantly. Add 6 cups of milk and 2 tablespoons soup base. Turn up heat and bring to a boil, whisking often until it starts to thicken. Turn down heat and simmer for a few minutes. Stir in rice, chicken, and corn and simmer for another few minutes. Next, stir in the heavy cream. If too thick, add more milk. Taste to see if more soup base is needed. Serve in bowls with parsley and a few almonds on top.

This is one of my favorite soup recipes. I love wild rice and the almonds on top are really fun. Serve with crusty bread for dunking. Hey, you can also use leftover turkey instead of chicken.   It's all good!

Southwest Turkey Soup

3 tablespoons olive oil

1 yellow onion, chopped

4 stalks celery, diced

1 green pepper, diced

1 teaspoon garlic salt

2 cans (4 ounces) diced green chilies

2 teaspoons chili powder

1 tablespoon ground cumin

2 garlic cloves, minced

1/2 teaspoon dried oregano leaves

1/4 teaspoon cayenne pepper (optional if you like it spicy)

4 to 6 cups chicken stock

1 can (15 ounces) black or pinto beans, drained and rinsed

1 can (14.5 ounces) diced tomatoes

2 to 3 cups cooked turkey, chopped or shredded

1 cup frozen corn, thawed

Fresh chopped fresh cilantro

Sour cream

Shredded monterey jack cheese

1 diced avocado

Fresh lime juice

Tortilla chips

Heat oil in large soup pan over medium heat. Add onion, celery, and bell pepper and cook a few minutes. Stir in garlic and cook another 30 seconds stirring constantly. Add garlic salt, chili powder, cumin, oregano and cayenne pepper. Stir in 4 to 5 cups chicken stock, tomatoes with juice and green chilies. Bring to a boil. Turn down heat a bit. Add turkey and corn and simmer for 5 to 10 minutes. If soup gets too thick or needs more broth, add more chicken stock. Ladle soup into bowls and serve with sour cream, cheese, cilantro, avocado, and a squeeze of fresh lime juice on top if you want. Great with tortilla chips or corn bread. I have a great cornbread recipe in the "What's on the Side?" chapter.

∞ ∞ ∞

I usually make this soup right after Thanksgiving. It's a great way to use up some of that leftover turkey. You can use chicken too. It's a really healthy soup if you take it easy on the toppings! You can also freeze this soup for up to 3 months. It's always great to have some soup in the freezer that you can pull out and heat in the microwave on those crazy, busy weeknights! Boy, have I had my share of those!! Thank goodness for the soup!

∞ ∞ ∞

Chicken Parmesan Soup

4 tablespoons olive oil

3 to 4 boneless, skinless chicken breast halves, diced into bite size pieces

2 teaspoons garlic salt

1/2 teaspoon black pepper

1 small onion, finely diced

3 cloves garlic, minced

1 can (28 ounces) crushed tomatoes

1 jar (26 ounces) marinara sauce

1 to 2 cups chicken stock

2 teaspoons sugar

2 teaspoons dried Italian seasoning

1 cup grated parmesan cheese, divided

Broken up spaghetti noodles, cooked

Garlic bread

Heat a large pot over medium-high heat with 2 tablespoons of oil. Season the chicken with garlic salt and pepper and add to pot. Cook for about 5 to 10 minutes, or until browned and cooked through. Remove from the pot and set aside. Add the other 2 tablespoons of oil along with onions. Sauté a few minutes until they start to get soft. Next, add the garlic and cook 30 seconds stirring constantly. Add chicken back to the pot, along with crushed tomatoes, 1 cup of stock, marinara sauce, sugar and Italian seasoning. Simmer for 10 to 20 minutes. Stir in 1/2 cup parmesan cheese. If soup gets too thick add a little more chicken stock or a little water. Serve soup in bowls over warm cooked spaghetti noodles with the extra grated parmesan cheese on top. Serve with warm garlic bread for dunking.

∾ ∾ ∾

This is a really fun soup that my kids love and yours will too! Even the really picky eaters! I came up with this one on a "snow day." I didn't want to run to the grocery store so I used the stuff we had in the fridge and pantry. It's so good, especially on a cold day! Warms you right up!

∾ ∾ ∾

∾ ∾ ∾

Riley, Ireland, and Levi, our dog, having fun on a snow day. What kid doesn't LOVE a snow day?

∾ ∾ ∾

Tortellini Soup

1 pound sweet or hot Italian sausage, casings removed

1½ cups onion, finely diced

1½ cups celery, finely diced

1 garlic teaspoon salt

Pinch of crushed red pepper flakes

2 to 3 cloves garlic, minced

6 to 8 cups chicken stock

1/2 cup dry red or white wine (optional)

1 can (28 ounces) diced tomatoes

2 teaspoons dried basil

1/2 teaspoon dried oregano

2 cups zucchini, diced

1 cup yellow summer squash, diced

20 ounces cheese tortellini

1/2 cup grated parmesan cheese

Fresh shredded parmesan cheese

In large soup pan fry sausage with onions and celery until sausage is crumbly and no longer pink. Add zucchini and summer squash and cook for another few minutes. Add garlic and cook for 30 seconds, stirring constantly. Season with garlic salt and a pinch of red pepper flakes. Stir in 6 cups stock, wine, tomatoes with juice, basil, and oregano. Bring to a boil. Reduce heat and simmer uncovered for a few minutes. Add tortellini and cook for another five minutes. Stir in grated parmesan cheese. If soup needs more broth add more chicken stock. Serve soup in bowls with shredded parmesan cheese on top.

⨍ ⨍ ⨍

This is another really great soup. Just warms you up all over on a cold winter day! Serve it with the "Amazing Cheese Bread" recipe in the first chapter of the book or just regular garlic bread and you've got a great dinner! This soup also freezes really well for up to 3 months.

⨍ ⨍ ⨍

Lasagna Soup

1½ pounds lean ground beef

1 medium onion, finely diced

2 to 3 cloves of garlic, minced

1/2 teaspoon oregano

2 teaspoons dried basil

1/2 teaspoon salt

Pinch of red pepper flakes

1 jar (26 ounces) marinara sauce

1 can (28 ounces) crushed tomatoes

1 tablespoon sugar

1 to 2 cups chicken stock

8 ounces mafalda (mini lasagna) or rotini pasta, cooked al dente

8 ounces ricotta cheese

1/4 cup grated parmesan

1/2 teaspoon garlic salt

Shredded mozzarella cheese

Chopped fresh basil or Italian parsley

In a large soup pan, brown the beef and onion together. Cook until beef is no longer pink, about 5 to 7 minutes. Drain any excess grease from the pan. Add the garlic, oregano, basil, salt and red pepper flakes and sauté for 30 seconds. Add crushed tomatoes, marinara sauce, sugar and 1 cup of stock. Bring to a boil. Simmer 5 to 10 minutes. Stir in cooked pasta. If too thick, add more stock. In a small bowl, combine the ricotta, parmesan and garlic salt. To serve, place a tablespoon or 2 of the ricotta mixture in each bowl. Ladle the soup on top. Serve with shredded mozzarella cheese and basil or parsley on top. Great with garlic bread for dunking.

∾ ∾ ∾

If your family likes lasagna, (and who doesn't?) you'll love this soup! It's another one I came up with one day. It's just fun and those mini lasagna noodles are too cute! Love that little cheesy surprise in the bottom of the bowl!

∾ ∾ ∾

Summer Minestrone

4 tablespoons olive oil, divided

1 medium onion, chopped

1 carrot, finely diced

3 celery stalks, diced

Salt and pepper

2 teaspoons dried basil

4 large garlic cloves, minced

2 medium sized zucchini, diced

1 medium yellow summer squash, diced

1 can (14 ounces) diced tomatoes, with juice

1 can (15 ounces) cannellini beans, drained and rinsed

8 ounces small shell pasta, cooked al dente

6 to 8 cups chicken stock

2 cups fresh spinach

Freshly grated parmesan

Heat 2 tablespoons of olive oil in large soup pan. Add the onion, carrots and celery. Cook for about 5 minutes until the vegetables start to soften. Add remaining 2 tablespoons olive oil, zucchini and summer squash. Season with some salt and pepper and the basil. Continue to cook for another few minutes. Add the garlic, and cook for another 30 seconds stirring constantly. Add the tomatoes, beans, and 6 cups of stock. Bring to a simmer and cook for a few minutes. Stir in pasta and spinach and cook another minute. Serve in soup bowls with parmesan cheese on top.

Even though I call it summer minestrone, I love this soup all year round because it's really good and really good for you! All those veggies! It's great in the summer with fresh veggies from the garden or, in my case, the farmer's market. Make sure to serve with bread for dunking. I LOVE to dunk!

Italian Wedding Soup

For Meatballs:

1 pound ground beef

1/2 cup seasoned Italian breadcrumbs

1 egg, beaten

1/4 cup grated parmesan cheese

2 clove garlic, minced

1 teaspoon garlic salt

1 teaspoon dried parsley

For Soup:

2 tablespoons olive oil

1½ cups onions, finely diced

1 cup carrots, finely diced

1½ cups celery, finely diced

2 cloves garlic, minced

Salt and pepper

8 to 10 cups chicken stock

3 cups fresh spinach

4 ounces Acini De Pepe pasta (little ball-shaped noodles)

Fresh grated parmesan cheese

Mix all meatball ingredients together in a large bowl. Form into tiny meatballs, about one inch in size. Bake meatballs in a large pan in a preheated 350 degree oven for 10 to 20 minutes until they are brown and cooked through. Meanwhile, while meatballs are baking, place olive oil in a large soup pan. Add onion, celery and carrots and cook on medium heat for about 5 minutes until they start to soften. Add garlic and cook for 30 seconds stirring constantly. Season with a little salt and pepper. Add 8 cups of stock and simmer for a few minutes. Add the pasta and simmer another 5 to 7 minutes. Add meatballs and fresh spinach and simmer another few minutes. Add more stock if needed. Season with salt and pepper taste. Serve soup in bowls with freshly grated parmesan cheese on top.

೮ ೮ ೮

I've been to a few big Italian weddings and they never served this soup. They should have, it's really good! I did some research and I guess it got its name because all the ingredients really work together, meaning they are "well married." Anyway, this is my version of this classic Italian soup. My kids love it and yours will too! Those little meatballs are so cute! Serve with crusty bread for dunking.

೮ ೮ ೮

Tuscan White Bean Soup

3 cans (15 ounces) white cannellini or great Northern beans, drained

3 tablespoons olive oil

1 onion, finely diced

2 carrots, peeled and finely diced

2 celery stalks, finely diced

Salt and pepper

1 large tomato, seeded and diced

1 cup chopped spinach

4 cloves of garlic, minced

1/4 teaspoon freshly ground black pepper

1 tablespoon finely chopped fresh rosemary, plus extra for the top

8 to 10 cups chicken or vegetable stock

Freshly grated parmesan cheese

Heat the oil in a large soup pan. Cook the onion, carrots and celery until they start to get soft. Season veggies with a little salt and pepper. Add the garlic and rosemary and cook for 30 seconds stirring constantly. Dump in the beans and 8 cups of stock. Bring to a boil, reduce the heat to low and simmer for about 20 minutes, stirring occasionally. Use a potato masher to mash up some of the beans. Stir in spinach and tomatoes and cook another minute or two. If too thick add more stock. Taste to see if more salt and pepper is needed. Serve in bowls with cheese and a little fresh rosemary on top.

Hungarian Sausage Soup

4 cups chicken stock

6 medium size potatoes, peeled and diced into one inch chunks

1 medium onion, chopped

1 can (28 ounces) diced tomatoes

2 cups sour cream, divided

1 ring of kielbasa, chopped into bite size pieces

1 tablespoon caraway seeds

Salt and pepper to taste

2 tablespoons chopped Italian parsley

In a big soup pan, add stock, potatoes, onion, tomatoes with juice and caraway seeds. Season with a little salt and pepper. Simmer for about 15 minutes. Add sausage and cook another 10 to 15 minutes until potatoes are tender. Turn down heat and whisk in one cup sour cream. Taste to see if more salt and pepper is needed. Serve in bowls with extra sour cream and chopped parsley on top. Great with rye or pumpernickel bread for dunking.

જી જી જી

This is probably one of the easiest soups I've ever made!! It's also one of the best!! It's just so different, so get out of your recipe rut and make this! I can't take credit for this one. Thanks to a great gal, Lonnie, who made it on my show. I hear it's an old family recipe.

જી જી જી

Reuben Soup

1 cup onion, finely diced

1 cup celery, finely diced

5 tablespoons butter

Salt and pepper

4 tablespoons flour

2 cups chicken stock

1½ cups finely chopped corned beef

1½ cups sauerkraut, drained

3 cups half and half

3 cups shredded Swiss cheese

3 tablespoons ketchup

2 tablespoons dill pickle relish

Chopped Italian parsley

Rye bread or rye croutons

In a large soup pan, cook onions and celery in butter until tender. Season with a little salt and pepper. Add flour and cook for another minute or two, stirring constantly. Add stock and bring to a boil, whisking often until it starts to thicken. Turn down heat a bit and stir in half and half, sauerkraut and corned beef. Add Swiss cheese, a handful at a time. Whisk until cheese is melted. Add ketchup and relish. Taste to see if more salt and pepper is needed. If soup gets too thick, add a little more stock, half and half, or milk. Serve with parsley on top. Great with rye bread for dunking or with rye croutons on top.

∾ ∾ ∾

I love a good Rueben sandwich, but I think I almost like this soup better. It's a great way to use up left over corned beef, which we seem to have a lot of after St. Patrick's Day. To make rye croutons, just cut some rye or pumpernickel bread into cubes. Drizzle with a little melted butter. Sprinkle with a little garlic salt and dried parsley and bake on a cookie sheet in a preheated 300 degree oven for 10 to 20 minutes until they get a little toasted and hard.

∾ ∾ ∾

Wisconsin Beer Cheese Soup

2 sticks butter

½ cup flour

1½ cups onion, finely diced

1½ cups celery, finely diced

1½ cups carrots, finely diced

2 cloves garlic, minced

1 bottle (12 ounces) beer

2 cups chicken stock

1 tablespoon Dijon mustard

6 to 8 cups half and half or milk (if you want it super rich and creamy, use half and half)

1/2 cup heavy cream

5 cups shredded sharp cheddar cheese

1 cup shredded Swiss cheese

A few dashes hot sauce

A couple dashes Worcestershire

Salt and pepper

Fresh chopped Italian parsley

Croutons or popcorn

In a large soup pan melt butter. Cook onion, celery, and carrot until they start to get soft. Season with salt and pepper. Add flour. Whisk constantly until it's well combined. Add beer, broth, and 6 cups of milk or half and half. Bring to a boil and simmer, whisking often until it starts to thicken. Add hot sauce, mustard, and Worcestershire. Add cheese, a handful at a time, whisking until it's smooth and creamy. Add 1/2 cup of heavy cream. If too thick add a little more milk, cream or half and half. Taste to see if more salt, pepper, or another dash of hot sauce is needed. Serve in bowls with parsley and croutons or popcorn on top. (Check out my recipe for homemade croutons in the "Super Salads" chapter.)

ᘛ ᘛ ᘛ

Okay, this soup is pure heaven! On one of those not-so-great days when you just want to throw in the towel, take a hot bath and make this soup! It will all be okay! Tomorrow is a new day! Want to spice up this soup? Use pepper jack cheese instead of Swiss. Sometimes I'll add a half pound of sliced smoked sausage to this soup. Either way it's TO DIE FOR! Start the diet tomorrow!

ᘛ ᘛ ᘛ

Mashed Potato Soup

1 pound bacon, chopped in small pieces

1 cup onion, finely diced

2 stalks celery, finely diced

2 to 3 cups milk

2 cups chicken stock

Salt and pepper

4 to 6 cups prepared mashed potatoes (leftover is great)

1/2 cup heavy cream

Shredded cheddar cheese

Scallions or chives chopped

Sour cream

In a large soup pan, fry bacon until crispy. Remove bacon from pan and set aside to crumble. Leave a couple of tablespoons of the bacon drippings in the pan. Cook celery and onions in the drippings until they start to get soft. Season with salt and pepper. Add 2 cups of milk and stock. Bring to a simmer. Stir in mashed potatoes and half of the crumbled bacon. Remove from heat and whisk in 1/4 cup heavy cream. Taste to see if more salt and pepper is needed. If mixture is too thick, add a little more milk or cream. Serve soup in bowls with scallions, remaining crumbled bacon, sour cream and cheddar cheese on top.

∽ ∽ ∽

Got leftover mashed potatoes? Don't throw them out! Make this soup! My daughter, Ireland, loves it, especially with lots of shredded cheese and bacon on top.   Plan ahead! Next time you're serving mashed potatoes make some extra. Then, turn them into this soup and you've got another great, super easy meal! I'm all about making things easy!

∽ ∽ ∽

Cheeseburger Chowder

1½ pounds ground beef

1/2 cup chopped celery

1/2 cup chopped onion

2 teaspoons garlic salt

1/2 teaspoon black pepper

4 tablespoons flour

4 to 6 cups milk

2 cups chicken stock

1 cup heavy cream

3 cups frozen southern style cubed hash browns or cooked diced potatoes

1 box (16 ounces) processed cheese, cut in cubes

Shredded cheddar cheese

Seeded and diced tomatoes

Chopped dill pickle

In large soup pan, brown beef. Add celery and onion. Cook until vegetables are tender and beef is no longer pink. Drain off any grease. Season with garlic salt and pepper. Stir in flour and cook for a minute or two. Add 4 cups of milk and stock. Bring to a boil, whisking often until it starts to thicken. Turn down heat to a low simmer. Stir in potatoes and cheese. Whisk until all cheese is melted. Add heavy cream. If too thick, add more milk. Taste to see if more salt and pepper is needed. Serve in bowls topped with extra cheese, diced tomato, and chopped dill pickle.

$$\infty \quad \infty \quad \infty$$

This soup is like a cheeseburger in a bowl. Creamy, cheesy and so good. Love the pickles and burger fixin's on top! It's just plain fun!

$$\infty \quad \infty \quad \infty$$

Spicy Corn and Crab Chowder

6 tablespoons butter

1 cup onion, finely diced

1 cup celery, finely diced

1 cup red bell pepper, finely diced

Salt and pepper

2 cloves garlic, minced

4 tablespoons flour

2 cups chicken stock

3 to 4 cups milk

2 teaspoons ground cumin

2 cups frozen southern style cubed hash browns

2 cups frozen corn, thawed or fresh corn off the cob

1 to 2 cups heavy cream

4 cups shredded pepper jack cheese, divided

2 cups imitation crabmeat, chopped

Freshly chopped cilantro

In a soup pan melt butter. Add onion and celery and cook on medium heat for a few minutes. Next add red pepper and cook another minute or two. Season with a little salt and pepper. Add garlic and cook for 30 seconds stirring constantly. Stir in cumin and flour. Cook for another minute or two stirring constantly until flour and vegetables are mixed well. Add stock and 3 cups of milk and bring to a boil, whisking often. When it starts to thicken, turn down heat and stir in potatoes. Add 3 cups of cheese, one handful at a time, whisking until cheese is melted. Stir in crabmeat, corn and one cup of heavy cream. Heat for a few minutes. If soup is too thick, add a little more milk or cream. Taste to see if more salt and pepper is needed. Serve in bowls with extra shredded cheese and fresh chopped cilantro on top.

∾ ∾ ∾

I love chowder, but this recipe is extra special! Especially when you can use fresh peaches n' cream corn (my favorite!) right from the cob! This is one of those rare times when imitation crabmeat works really well. If you can't take the heat, use monterey jack cheese instead of pepper jack- it will still be just as good!

∾ ∾ ∾

Super Simple White Chicken Chili

1 onion, diced

1 green pepper, diced

3 tablespoons olive oil

2 teaspoons garlic salt

1/2 teaspoon black pepper

2 jars (48 ounces) or 6 cans (15 ounces) Great Northern Beans, drained

4 boneless, skinless chicken breast halves, cooked and shredded

4 cups chicken stock

2 cans (4 ounces) diced green chiles

1 jar (16 ounces) chunky green or red salsa or picante sauce (I like to use the green salsa)

2 tablespoons ground cumin

Your favorite chili fixin's

In a big pot, heat olive oil and sauté onion and green pepper for a few minutes until they start to get soft. Season with garlic salt and pepper. Dump the rest of the ingredients in the pot. Simmer on low to medium heat for 20 to 30 minutes. You can also put this all in a slow cooker and heat on low for 2 to 3 hours. If it gets too thick, add a little water or chicken stock. Serve with your favorite chili fixin's.

∾ ∾ ∾

I really like chili, but sometimes it doesn't like me, if you know what I mean! That's why I fell in love with white chicken chili. Much easier on the tummy!!

∾ ∾ ∾

Taco Soup

2 pounds ground beef or ground turkey

1 medium yellow onion, finely diced

1 green pepper, finely diced (optional)

1 packet (1.25 ounces) taco seasoning

1 packet (1 ounce) dry ranch dressing mix

1 can (28 ounces) diced or crushed tomatoes

1 jar (16 ounces) salsa

1 can (4 ounces) diced green chiles

2 cups chicken stock

1 can (15 ounces) ranch style beans

2 cups frozen or 1 can (15 ounces) whole kernel corn, drained

In a large soup pan brown the beef and onion and pepper until beef is crumbly and no longer pink. Drain any grease. Add next 7 ingredients. Simmer for 15 to 25 minutes. If soup needs more broth add a little water or chicken stock. Serve with your favorite taco fixings and tortilla chips for dunking.

∾ ∾ ∾

This is a super quick and easy soup recipe. Brown the beef and just dump it all in. Dinner's ready in less than 30 minutes. A lot of times that's quicker than ordering a pizza! If the kids don't like beans or green pepper, leave them out. I know they like tacos, so they'll love this soup!

∾ ∾ ∾

Posole (Mexican Pork Stew)

4 tablespoons olive oil

1 cup onion, diced

1 cup celery, diced

1 cup green pepper, finely diced

4 cloves garlic, minced

1 tablespoon cumin

1/2 teaspoon Mexican or regular oregano

1 jar (16 ounces) green salsa

2 cans (4 ounces) diced green chiles

4 to 6 cups chicken stock

2 to 3 cups cooked and shredded pork

3 cans (15 ounces) white hominy, rinsed and drained (find it near the canned corn)

Salt and pepper

Lime wedges

Sour cream

Diced avocados

Diced fresh or pickled jalapeno peppers

Chopped cilantro

Chopped scallions

Shredded monterey jack cheese

Heat oil in a large soup pan. Add onion, celery, and green pepper and cook about 5 minutes until they start get soft. Season with a little salt and pepper. Add garlic and cook for 30 seconds, stirring constantly. Add cumin, oregano, 4 to 6 cups chicken stock, salsa, green chiles, pork and hominy and simmer for 10 to 20 minutes. Add salt and pepper to taste. If too thick, add more stock or some water. To serve, ladle posole into bowls. Great with a little squeeze of lime juice on top! Put all the toppings out let everyone spoon on their favorites.

∾ ∾ ∾

Posole, also spelled Pozole, is a Mexican soup or stew served traditionally during the holidays. I love it! You can make it with shredded chicken instead of pork. It's great either way. If you make my Garlic Pork Roast in the "Just Throw it in the Slow Cooker" chapter, use some of the leftovers to make this. I think you'll really love it, especially with all the fun toppings. Just something a little different from chili.

∾ ∾ ∾

BREAKFAST & BRUNCH TIME

My Absolute Favorite Make Ahead Brunch Bake

1 box or bag (6 ounces) garlic croutons

4 cups sharp shredded cheddar cheese, divided

1 pound bulk breakfast sausage, cooked and crumbled

3/4 teaspoon dry mustard

4 eggs

3¾ cups milk, divided

1 can (10.75 ounces) cream of mushroom soup

1 bag (32 ounces) country style shredded frozen hash browns, thawed

1 teaspoon paprika

Place croutons in the bottom of a 9" × 13" baking dish that has been sprayed with cooking spray. Sprinkle 1 cup of the cheese over croutons. Next, spoon the sausage over the cheese. In a large bowl whisk together eggs, mustard and 2¼ cups milk. Pour egg mixture over sausage. Cover and refrigerate over night. The next morning, whisk together soup and 1½ cups of milk. Uncover your baking dish and spoon the soup mixture over the top. Next, sprinkle on the hashbrowns. Top with remaining 3 cups cheese and paprika. Baked loosely covered with foil in a preheated 350 degree oven for 50 to 60 minutes. Uncover and bake another 15 to 20 minutes until eggs are set and cheese is bubbly. Wait 5 to 10 minutes before cutting into squares and serving.

This is a really special recipe! It came to me from a very special lady who is no longer with us. It's my go-to recipe on holiday mornings or when we have company visiting. It's great because you make most of it ahead of time, park it in the fridge and then bake it up in the morning. The mushroom soup makes it extra good! This recipe is so good that I caught my sister in-law eating the leftovers cold out of the fridge the day after Christmas. Too funny! I like to serve this with fresh fruit and something sweet, like muffins or coffee cake. Knowing me I'd pick up the fruit and hit the grocery store bakery. Hey, you can't to it all and you don't have too!" Thanks Arlene! I miss you and think of you every time I make this.

Italian Brunch Bake

1 box or bag (6 ounces) seasoned croutons

1 pound sweet Italian sausage, casings removed

1 cup onion, finely diced

1 cup red bell pepper, finely diced

2 cups diced zucchini, finely diced

1/2 cup grated parmesan cheese, divided

4 cups shredded fontina or mozzarella cheese, divided

6 eggs

3 cups milk

1/2 teaspoon garlic salt

1/2 teaspoon freshly ground black pepper

Spray a 9" x 13" pan with cooking spray. Spread croutons evenly in bottom of dish. In a skillet, brown sausage with onion over medium-high heat until no longer pink, breaking up any large pieces. Add red pepper and zucchini. Cook for another couple minutes, until vegetables begin to soften a bit. To assemble strata, spoon sausage and vegetables evenly over croutons. Top with 1 cup shredded cheese. In a large bowl whisk together eggs, milk, 1/4 cup parmesan cheese, garlic salt and pepper. Pour egg mixture over sausage and vegetables. Cover well with foil and refrigerate overnight. When you are ready to bake, preheat the oven to 350 degrees. Sprinkle remaining 3 cups fontina or mozzarella cheese on top. Then sprinkle parmesan cheese on top of that. Cover loosely with foil. Bake 50 to 60 minutes covered until eggs are set. Uncover and bake another 15 to 20 minutes. Let stand 5 to 10 minutes before slicing into squares and serving.

Ham and Cheese Strata

1 loaf French bread, cut in cubes

1/2 pound deli or leftover ham, diced

3 cups shredded cheddar cheese

1 cup shredded Swiss cheese

6 eggs

3 cups milk

1/2 teaspoon garlic salt

3/4 teaspoon dry mustard

1/4 teaspoon black pepper

2 cups crushed corn flakes

1/2 cup butter, melted

Spray a 9" × 13" baking dish with cooking spray. Spread half of bread cubes evenly in dish. Add ham and both cheeses. Cover with remaining bread cubes. In a bowl, whisk together eggs, milk and spices. Pour mixture evenly over bread, ham and cheese. Cover with foil and refrigerate overnight. Before baking, combine cornflakes and butter for topping. Spread evenly over strata. Bake loosely covered with foil in a preheated a 350 oven for 50 to 60 minutes. Uncover and bake another 15 to 20 minutes until the eggs are completely set and the top is golden. Wait 5 to 10 minutes before cutting into squares and serving.

Bacon, Mushroom and Swiss Bake

3 tablespoons butter

2 packages (8 ounces) fresh mushrooms, sliced

5 large (5 inch) croissants, torn into small pieces

1 pound bacon, cooked and crumbled

2 cups shredded Swiss Cheese, divided

6 eggs

1 cup milk

2 tablespoons Dijon mustard

2 tablespoons fresh tarragon, chopped

1/2 teaspoon salt

1/2 teaspoon pepper

Heat butter in large skillet over medium high heat. Add mushrooms, sauté 2 to 3 minutes or until slightly softened; cool and drain. In large bowl, combine croissant pieces, bacon, 1 cup Swiss cheese and sautéed mushrooms. In medium bowl, whisk together eggs, milk, Dijon mustard, tarragon, salt and pepper. Pour egg mixture over croissant mixture. Toss and spoon into a 9" × 13" baking dish that has been sprayed with cooking spray. Sprinkle with remaining 1 cup Swiss cheese, cover with foil. Can be refrigerated for up to 24 hours, if you want. Preheat oven to 350 degrees. Bake covered for 30 minutes. Uncover and bake 15 to 20 more minutes or until golden and puffed. Let stand 10 minutes before slicing into squares and serving.

Bacon, Egg and Cheese Breakfast Bake

1 tube (8 ounces) crescent roll dough (We love the garlic flavored, but the seamless dough works great too!)

3 cups shredded cheddar cheese

8 eggs

1 pound of bacon, cooked, and crumbled

Salt and pepper

Press crescent dough into a 9" × 13" pan that has been sprayed with cooking spray. Press dough a little up each side of the pan. Try and press the seams together if you aren't using the seamless dough. Sprinkle cheese and bacon over the dough. In a bowl whisk together eggs and a little salt and pepper. Bake at 350 for 30 to 45 minutes until eggs are set. Wait a few minutes and slice into squares.

Ꮿ Ꮿ Ꮿ

Okay, it doesn't get much easier than this!! Need a nice breakfast and you just didn't get a chance to do one of my make-aheads? Here you go! This is perfect! It's Ireland's favorite. She's a bacon lover! Must take after her mom! But, hey you can use cooked sausage or diced ham too! It's all good!

Ꮿ Ꮿ Ꮿ

Breakfast Pizza

8 slices of bacon, cooked and crumbled

1 tube (13.8 ounces) refrigerated pizza dough

8 eggs

1/4 cup milk

Salt and pepper

2 tablespoons butter

1/2 cup (4 ounces) plain or chive and onion cream cheese, softened

2 cups shredded cheddar cheese

1 tablespoon chopped chives or Italian parsley

Press out pizza crust on a pizza pan that has been sprayed with cooking spray. In a big bowl whisk together eggs, milk, salt and pepper. Melt butter in a large non-stick skillet. Put egg mixture in the skillet. Let the eggs start to set up a bit and then scramble. Don't overcook the eggs. They should be a little soft. Spread cream cheese on top of the crust. Spoons eggs on top. Next, sprinkle on bacon and shredded cheese. Bake in preheated 425 degree oven for 12 to 20 minutes until crust is golden and cheese is melted. Sprinkle chives or parsley on top. Cut into wedges like a pizza and serve right away.

Pizza for breakfast? Why not! Especially this one! My son Riley is a total pizza nut!
He could and would eat pizza everyday for breakfast, lunch, and dinner if I let him.
We once went on a pizza vacation in Chicago. The plan was to spend a week there.
We'd go to museums, shop, hang out and eat at a bunch of different pizza places
all over the city. Then, we'd all decide which places we liked best. Well, the trip got
cut short after poor Riley came down with pneumonia on the 2nd day. BUMMER!
We were just getting started. Sure hope we can do it again some day! Until then
I just make a lot of pizza!

My teenage son Riley, hanging out on the dock on Walloon Lake in Michigan. He
loves to read, run and eat pizza!

Ham and Egg Braid

4 eggs

1/4 cup milk

Salt and pepper

1 tablespoon butter

2 tablespoons chopped red

2 tablespoons chopped scallions

2 ounces of cream cheese, cut in small cubes

4 to 6 thin slices of ham

1 cup shredded Swiss or cheddar cheese

1 tube (8 ounces) crescent roll dough

1 teaspoon dried parsley

Place a large piece of parchment paper or foil that has been sprayed with cooking spray on a cookie sheet or jelly roll pan. Open the tube of dough and unroll it on the parchment or foil. If you are not using seamless dough, press the seams together. Next, use a rolling pin or your hands to roll or press out the dough just a bit to form a big rectangle. Use a knife or kitchen scissors to make 1 inch slices all the way down each side of the longest side of the dough. This should leave about a 3 inch area in the middle of the dough for your filling. Separate one egg. Set aside the egg white. Whisk the yolk from that egg along with the 3 other eggs and milk together. Season with a little salt and pepper. Heat butter in a non-stick pan. Add egg mixture. Let the eggs start to set a bit and then scramble and add the red pepper, scallions, and pieces of cream cheese. Cook until eggs are still a little soft. Don't overcook the eggs! Place ham, overlapping the slices, down the middle of the dough. Spoon cooked eggs on top of ham. Sprinkle cheese over eggs. To braid, lift the strips of dough across the filling to meet the center. Brush egg white over the braid. Sprinkle with parsley. Cook in a preheated 400 degree oven for 20 to 30 minutes until the pastry is golden. Carefully transfer the braid to a large platter. Cut into 2 inch strips and serve.

Brunch Stromboli

1 pound loaf frozen bread dough, thawed

2 tablespoons butter, melted

1/4 teaspoon garlic salt

1/4 pound thinly sliced deli ham or turkey, or a little of both

6 bacon strips, cooked and crumbled

6 thin slices of mozzarella cheese

6 thin slices American or cheddar cheese

On a baking sheet sprayed with non-stick cooking spray, roll dough into a large 10" × 14" rectangle. In a small bowl, combine the butter and garlic salt. Brush dough with half of the butter mixture. Layer the ham or turkey, mozzarella cheese, bacon and cheddar cheese lengthwise over half of the dough to within 1/2 inch of edges. Fold dough over and pinch firmly to seal. Brush with remaining butter mixture. Bake at 400 degrees for 10 to 12 minutes or until golden brown. Cut into 2 inch slices and serve while still warm.

෴ ෴ ෴

This is a fun one! If you have someone who doesn't do eggs (my son Riley's not a big fan), this is perfect! It's a really quick fix too! Serve it with a fresh fruit salad and call it a day! This actually is great to serve for dinner too!

෴ ෴ ෴

Elegant Eggs and Ham in Puff Pastry

1 package (10 ounces) frozen puff pastry shells

6 tablespoons butter, divided

3 tablespoons flour

1½ to 2 cups milk

1½ cups shredded sharp cheddar cheese

1/4 cup heavy cream

Dash hot sauce

1/2 teaspoon dry mustard

8 to 10 eggs

1/4 cup water

Salt and pepper

6 slices thin deli ham, warmed

2 tablespoons chopped fresh chives or Italian parsley (optional)

Bake pastry shells according to package directions. Melt 4 tablespoons of butter in a saucepan. Add flour and whisk until smooth. Gradually stir in 1½ cups milk. Cook until it thickens. Whisk in cheese, hot sauce, mustard and cream. Season with salt and pepper. If sauce gets too thick, add more milk. Beat eggs and water in bowl. Season with salt and pepper. Heat remaining 2 tablespoons of butter in a skillet. Add eggs and scramble over low heat. Split pastry shells in half and place bottom halves on plates. Top each with a slice of ham, scrambled eggs and put pastry shell tops on. Spoon some cheese sauce on top and sprinkle with fresh chives or parsley. Makes 6.

෴ ෴ ෴

Want to really impress! Make these for breakfast or brunch! They are so easy but nobody will ever know! They are even kid friendly! Serve them with a little fresh fruit on the side. Just really elegant! (LOVE that word! Don't get a chance to use it much!)

෴ ෴ ෴

Quiche Lorraine

1 (9 inch) deep dish pie crust in tin or plate

8 slices bacon, diced into 1 inch pieces

1/2 cup onion, finely diced

1 cup shredded gruyere cheese

3 eggs

1½ cups heavy cream

1/4 teaspoon salt

1/4 teaspoon dry mustard

1/4 teaspoon freshly grounded black pepper

Pinch of nutmeg

1 tablespoon fresh chopped chives or Italian parsley

In a medium skillet, sauté bacon over medium heat until the bacon just starts to get a little crisp. Remove bacon to a plate and use a paper towel to soak up grease. Cook onion in a little of the bacon grease until soft. Sprinkle bacon and onion on bottom of pie crust. Add gruyere cheese. In a medium bowl whisk together eggs, heavy cream, salt, dry mustard, nutmeg and black pepper. Pour mixture into crust. Bake on a cookie sheet in a preheated 350 degree oven for 40 to 60 minutes or until a knife inserted in the center comes out clean. Check at 40 minutes and be careful not to over bake. If the edges of the crust start to get too brown you can cover them with foil. Cool quiche for about ten minutes. Sprinkle quiche with chives or parsley and cut into wedges to serve.

Seafood Quiche

9 inch deep dish pie shell, in tin or plate

2 tablespoons butter

1/2 pound uncooked medium size shrimp, peeled and deveined

1/4 teaspoon garlic salt

1/4 teaspoon dried dill

Juice from a quarter of a lemon

3 eggs

1½ cups heavy cream

1/4 teaspoon Worcestershire sauce

1/4 teaspoon black pepper

1 can (4.25 ounces) lump crab meat, drained

2 cups shredded Swiss cheese

2 tablespoons chopped scallions

1 tablespoon fresh chopped dill or Italian parsley

In a skillet melt butter. Cook shrimp in butter until it just starts to turn pink. Season shrimp with garlic salt and dill. Squeeze a little fresh lemon juice on top. In a bowl whisk together eggs, cream, Worcestershire and pepper. Place crabmeat, shrimp, half of the cheese and the scallions on the bottom of the uncooked pie shell, pour egg mixture over top. Top with rest of cheese.   Bake on a cookie sheet in a preheated 350 degree oven for 40 to 60 minutes or until a knife inserted in the center comes out clean. Check at 40 minutes and be careful not to over bake. If the edges of the crust start to get too brown you can cover them with foil. Cool quiche for about ten minutes. Sprinkle quiche with fresh dill or parsley and cut into wedges to serve.

If you like seafood, and you like quiche, you're going to love this! I had a piece of seafood quiche as an appetizer at a fancy dinner party and I just had to find a way to make it at home. So, here you go! Just something special!

Make Ahead Breakfast Burritos

18 eggs

1/2 cup milk or water

Salt and pepper

3 to 4 tablespoons butter

1 pound bulk breakfast sausage, cooked and crumbled

1 bag (32 ounces) frozen hash brown potatoes, southern style cubed or O'Brien, thawed

3 to 4 cups shredded cheddar cheese

12 large (10" to 12" burrito size) flour tortillas (you can use smaller 8" flour tortillas too but then you'll need more of them)

Tin foil

Whisk together the eggs with milk or water. Season with salt and pepper. In a really big non-stick skillet melt butter. Scramble the eggs and still they are still a little soft. Don't overcook the eggs! Place hash browns, scrambled eggs, cheese and sausage in a big bowl. Toss gently. Heat a few of the flour tortillas at a time in the microwave for 10 to 15 seconds to soften. Remove from microwave. Place a couple of big spoonfuls of the potato-egg-sausage-cheese mixture down the center of each tortilla. Fold burrito, folding the short ends in first and wrapping the long ends around. Wrap each burrito individually in tin foil. Repeat process using all the tortillas. You put the burritos in resealable plastic gallon size bags and freeze them. When you're ready to eat, take the number you need out of the freezer the night before and let them thaw in the refrigerator overnight. Place them in a preheated 350 degree oven for about 20 to 25 minutes until they're heated through. You can also take them out of the freezer in the morning, take the foil off and heat in the microwave. Serve with sour cream and salsa if you want. These keep in the freezer for about 2 months. You can also use a smaller size flour tortilla for a smaller appetite and then this recipe will make even more breakfast burritos, depending on the size tortilla you're using.

Do your kids get tired of toast and cereal in the morning? I know mine do! Especially Ireland! She loves a nice, hot breakfast! I absolutely LOVE this recipe. Make this on a Sunday (my usual big cooking day). You can have them for breakfast and then freeze the rest. Then, when you or the kiddos are wanting something warm for breakfast, no problem! Homemade breakfast burritos right in your freezer. Keeps my family from hitting the drive-thru places for breakfast too. And, if you're running late you can even have the kids eat these on the bus (if the bus driver is okay with that. Don't want to get anybody in trouble!) or in the car. How cool is that! And, once again mom or dad looks like a rock star! LOVE IT!

Blueberry Pecan Baked French Toast

1 large loaf French bread, cut into 2 inch cubes

6 eggs

3 cups milk

1/2 teaspoon cinnamon

1 teaspoon vanilla

1½ cups brown sugar, divided

1 cup pecans

1/4 cup butter

Pinch of salt

2 cups blueberries

Maple syrup or blueberry syrup (optional)

Spray a 9" × 13" baking dish with cooking spray. Place bread in the baking dish. In a large bowl whisk together eggs, milk, cinnamon, vanilla and 1/2 cup brown sugar and pour evenly over bread. Chill covered in the fridge overnight. When ready to bake, preheat the oven to 350. Sprinkle pecans and blueberries evenly over bread mixture. Next sprinkle 1 cup of brown sugar over the top. Cut the butter into small pieces and scatter it on top of the brown sugar. Bake loosely covered with foil for about 50 to 60 minutes. Uncover and bake another 15 to 25 minutes until all liquid is absorbed and the top is golden and bubbly. Let cool a few minutes before cutting in squares and serving. Serve with warm maple or blueberry syrup if you want, but it doesn't really need it.

$$\backsim \quad \backsim \quad \backsim$$

This is amazing!! You just HAVE to make it! If the kids don't do nuts, leave them out. No biggie! Just remember you need to put most of this recipe together the day before you want to serve it. When company is coming and you really want to "WOW" them, this will do it!

$$\backsim \quad \backsim \quad \backsim$$

Raspberry 'n Cream Baked French Toast

1 cup maple syrup

1 large French bread, cut into 2 inch cubes

1 package (8 ounces) cream cheese, cut in small cubes

3 cups milk

6 eggs

1/2 teaspoon cinnamon

1 teaspoon vanilla

1½ to 2 cups fresh raspberries

3/4 cup brown sugar

3 to 4 tablespoons butter

Extra maple syrup or raspberry syrup (optional)

Spray a 9" x 13" baking dish with cooking spray. Pour 1 cup of maple syrup into the baking dish, spreading in an even layer. Add half of the bread cubes in the bottom of the dish. Place half of the raspberries and half of the cubes of the cream cheese over the layer of bread. Whisk together eggs, milk, cinnamon, and vanilla. Pour the egg mixture over the bread. Now put the rest of the bread cubes on top and push the bread down a bit to soak up the bread mixture on top. Top with remaining cream cheese and raspberries. Cover with foil and place in refrigerator overnight. When ready to bake, preheat the oven to 350 degrees. Uncover casserole and sprinkle brown sugar on the top. Dot small pieces of butter over the top of the brown sugar. Cover loosely with foil. Bake for 50 to 60 minutes. Remove foil and bake another 15 to 25 minutes until all the liquid is absorbed and the top is bubbly. Let cool a few minutes before cutting into squares and serving. You can serve this with maple or raspberry syrup but you don't have to!

Peaches 'n Cream Baked French Toast

1 big loaf French bread, cut in 2 inch cubes

1 cup maple syrup

3 cups fresh or frozen sliced peaches

1 package (8 ounces) cream cheese, cut in small cubes

6 eggs

3 cups milk

1 teaspoon vanilla

1/2 teaspoon cinnamon

3/4 cup brown sugar

3 to 4 tablespoons butter

1/4 cup sliced almonds (completely optional!)

Extra maple syrup and or whipped cream (optional)

Spray a 9" × 13" pan with cooking spray. Pour syrup into the dish and spread it out evenly. Place half of the bread in the dish. Next sprinkle half of the peaches and half of the cream cheese cubes on top of the bread. Whisk together eggs, milk, cinnamon, and vanilla. Pour over the bread. Next, place the rest of the bread cubes on top. Push bread down a bit to soak up egg mixture. Top with remaining peaches and cream cheese. Cover well and refrigerate overnight. Before baking uncover and sprinkle with brown sugar and dot with small pieces of butter. Bake loosely covered in foil in a preheated 350 degree oven for 50 to 60 minutes. Uncover and sprinkle on almonds if you like nuts and bake another 15 to 25 minutes until all the liquid is absorbed and top is golden. Let cool a few minutes before cutting into squares. Serve with warm maple syrup or a little whipped cream if you want. Come on, you know you do! I love whipped cream!!

Oven Baked Oatmeal

1½ cups quick cooking oatmeal

1/3 cup brown sugar

1/2 cup dried cherries, cranberries, apples or raisins

1/2 cup walnuts (optional)

1/2 teaspoon cinnamon

1/2 teaspoon almond or maple extract

1 teaspoon vanilla

2 cups milk

1 cup water

Mix all ingredients together. Spoon into an 8" × 8" pan or small casserole dish that has been sprayed with cooking spray. Bake in a preheated 350 degree oven for about 20 minutes. You can serve with milk and extra brown sugar on top if you'd like.

∾ ∾ ∾

I got this recipe from a gal I work with. Everyone loves it, especially on those super cold winter days!! Warms you right up. Thanks Terri!

∾ ∾ ∾

Quick and Easy Coffee Cake

Topping:

1/2 cup brown sugar

1/4 cup flour

1/4 cup butter, room temperature

1 teaspoon cinnamon

Cake:

1½ cups flour

2½ teaspoons baking powder

1/2 teaspoon salt

1 egg, beaten

3/4 cup sugar

1/3 cup melted butter

1/2 cup milk

1 teaspoon vanilla

In small mixing bowl, combine topping ingredients. Blend with fork until crumbly. Set aside. For the cake, mix 1½ cups flour with baking powder and salt into a bowl. In another bowl, mix together egg, 3/4 cup sugar and 1/3 cup melted butter. Add milk and vanilla. Stir in flour mixture and mix well. Spoon cake batter into a buttered and floured 8" × 8" pan. Sprinkle crumb topping mixture evenly over the batter. Bake at 375 for 20 to 30 minutes, or until a knife inserted in the center comes out clean. Gotta serve this warm, right out of the oven, maybe with a little butter on top too. Oh yeah!

Basic Morning Muffin Mix

2 cups all purpose flour

2/3 cup sugar (or more if you like your muffins a little sweeter or if you're adding tart fruit)

1/2 teaspoon salt

1 tablespoon baking powder

1 cup milk

1/4 cup vegetable oil

2 large eggs

Preheat oven to 400 degrees. Blend together the dry ingredients. In another bowl, beat the milk, oil and eggs together. Pour wet ingredients into dry ingredients. Gently mix. The batter should be a little lumpy. Here's where you can have some fun and jazz up this mix the way you want to. Fold in 1½ cups fresh or frozen fruit, like blueberries, raspberries, cranberries, diced peaches, etc. You can also add chocolate chips or nuts. Line a muffin pan with cupcake liners and fill them about two-thirds of the way full. Place muffins in the oven and bake for 15 to 20 minutes. Makes 12 regular size muffins or 24 mini-muffins. Go for it! Make them your way!

ᨀ ᨀ ᨀ

My daughter Ireland LOVES muffins! Especially warm out of the oven! (okay who doesn't?) Anyway, this is a really easy basic muffin recipe. Now it's up to you to make whatever kind of muffins you're in the mood for. We love to add fresh blueberries and lemon zest, or cranberries and orange zest. Or, diced apples and cinnamon! Then, when they come out of the oven you can dip the muffin tops in melted butter and sprinkle a little sugar or cinnamon or both on top. Go crazy! If I can do these, you can too. Trust me! I don't bake much! If it's not easy, it's not happening! This is easy!

ᨀ ᨀ ᨀ

Orange Sticky Rolls

1/2 cup brown sugar

4 tablespoons butter

2 teaspoons orange zest

4 tablespoons orange juice

1 tube (8 ounces) crescent rolls (I love the seamless dough!)

Preheat oven to 350 degrees. Spray an 8" or 9" round pan with cooking spray. In a small pan heat brown sugar, butter, orange zest and juice. Cook and stir over medium heat until bubbly. Set aside. Remove dough from can but don't unroll it. Cut it into 8 slices. Arrange slices flat in pan. Spoon brown sugar mixture evenly over slices. Bake for 12 to 15 minutes or until golden brown. Serve warm.

∾ ∾ ∾

This is why you always need to have a few tubes of crescent rolls in your fridge!! You can whip these up in no time. They make a great sweet breakfast treat to go with all the egg bake recipes earlier in this chapter.

∾ ∾ ∾

Easy Monkey Bread

4 cans (7.5 ounces) refrigerated biscuits (Get a 4 pack! It's usually cheaper!)

1 cup brown sugar

1½ sticks butter

1/2 cup white sugar

1 teaspoon cinnamon

Preheat oven to 350 degrees and spray a bundt or tube pan with cooking spray. Mix white sugar and cinnamon in a medium sized plastic bag. Cut the biscuits in quarters and place six to eight biscuit pieces in the sugar cinnamon mix. Shake well. Arrange pieces in the bottom of the greased pan. Continue layering until all the biscuit pieces are coated and in the pan. In a small saucepan, melt the butter with the brown sugar over medium heat. Boil for 1 minute. Pour over the layered biscuits. Bake for 35 minutes. Let bread cool in pan for 10 minutes, and then turn out onto a place. Pull apart and enjoy!

❧ ❧ ❧

This is a super fun recipe! I smile every time I make it. I smile even more when I pull off and eat a piece. Have the kids help with this one! Just heavenly warm out of the oven! So easy, and super cheap to make too!

❧ ❧ ❧

NO MORE BORING SANDWICHES

Garden Veggie Wrap

1 package (8 ounces) cream cheese, softened

2 tablespoons chopped scallions

2 tablespoons chopped fresh dill or 2 teaspoons dried dill

2 teaspoons garlic salt

8 to 10 inch spinach tortillas

baby spinach

thinly sliced cucumber

thinly sliced red onion

thinly sliced tomatoes

Mix together first 4 ingredients to make an herb cream cheese spread. Spread a few tablespoons of the cream cheese mixture on tortilla. Top with veggies (don't over stuff) and wrap tightly. Slice wrap on an angle and enjoy! Cream cheese spread keeps in the fridge for up to a week.

∽ ∽ ∽

Wraps rock! You know why? Well, because unlike most sandwiches, you can make them in the morning, wrap them up, and they don't get mushy. I HATE WHEN THAT HAPPENS! I had a sandwich like this at a restaurant near our cottage. I think I paid 8 bucks for it. Then I thought, I can totally make these at home. So, I do! Love to pack it up and take it to the beach in the summer! Which is my absolute FAVORITE thing to do in the whole wide world! Take the kids to the beach near our cottage, bring a great sandwich, and a good book, it just doesn't get much better!!! I bring Levi, the dog, too and leave Bob at home. He hates the beach! (typical guy, right?)

∽ ∽ ∽

Turkey Club Wrap

1   8 to 10 inch plain or flavored tortilla

2 to 3 tablespoons prepared ranch dressing or mayonnaise

A few slices of deli turkey breast

2 slices crispy cooked bacon

1/4 cup shredded cheddar cheese

2 to 3 slices of tomato

1 few slices ripe avocado (optional)

1 to 2 large leaves of lettuce

Salt and pepper

Spread wrap with ranch dressing or mayonnaise. Top with remaining ingredients. Season with a little salt and pepper. Roll up and slice on an angle.

෨ ෨ ෨

Here's another great wrap recipe. Did I mention I love wraps? This is Bob's favorite!

෨ ෨ ෨

Excellent Egg Salad Sandwiches

8 hard-boiled eggs, peeled and chopped

1 tablespoon finely diced red onion

1/4 cup finely diced celery

1/2 cup mayonnaise

1/2 teaspoon garlic salt

Fresh ground black pepper to taste

2 tablespoons chopped fresh dill

Slices of sourdough, pumpernickel or whole grain bread

Leaf lettuce

Mix together first 7 ingredients. If the salad seems a little dry add some more mayonnaise. Serve on bread (I like mine toasted) with a piece of leaf lettuce. Makes about 4 to 6 sandwiches.

∽ ∽ ∽

When's the last time you had a really good egg salad sandwich? I mean, come on, there's nothing better! Boil some eggs and make this! It's really good! Don't have fresh dill? No big deal, use a half teaspoon or so of dried. It's all good!

∽ ∽ ∽

Baked Tuna Melt

2 cans (5 ounces) albacore tuna packed in water, drained well and flaked

1/4 cup celery, finely diced

1/4 cup red pepper, finely diced

1/2 cup mayonnaise

1 teaspoon garlic powder

1/4 teaspoon black pepper

1 teaspoon fresh lemon juice

2 tablespoons chopped fresh dill

1 loaf crusty French bread, sliced in half

2 cups shredded cheddar cheese

1 to 2 sliced tomatoes

Preheat oven to 350 degrees. Mix together first 8 ingredients. If too dry, add a little more mayonnaise. Pull a little of the inside of both sides of the bread out. Spoon the tuna mixture into one piece of the French bread. Top with cheese and tomatoes. Place the other piece of bread on top. Wrap foil around the sandwich and bake for 20 to 30 minutes. Cut into 2 to 4 inch pieces and serve warm.

৩ ৩ ৩

I've been making this for years. Everybody loves it! I think it's way better then your typical tuna melt! The French bread gets really crunchy and the cheese gets all melted. Okay, I'm getting hungry just thinking about it! Gotta serve this with potato chips!! Makes a great quick 'n easy weeknight dinner!

৩ ৩ ৩

Baked Hot Ham and Cheese Sandwiches

1 stick softened butter

1 cup mayonnaise

1/2 teaspoon garlic salt

1 to 2 tablespoons Dijon mustard (if you don't like mustard, leave it out)

8 to 12 hard rolls (I like the poppy seed, but the kids like plain)

1½ to 2 pounds shaved deli ham

8 to 12 slices Swiss cheese

Tin foil

Mix the first 4 ingredients. Spread mixture generously on both sides of buns. Next add some ham and 1 slice of cheese to make the sandwiches. Wrap each sandwich in foil. Bake them on a cookie sheet in a preheated 325 degree oven for 12 to 15 minutes until buns get toasted, and cheese is melted. You can also cook these on the grill, indirect heat, meaning not directly on the hot coals or gas flame.

∾ ∾ ∾

Bored with the "Same Old" ham sandwich? Give these a try! They make a super quick dinner on those crazy weeknights we all have! These rock if you are tailgating!! Take them pre-made to a game and throw them on the grill. YUM!

∾ ∾ ∾

Baked Club Sandwich

1 tube (11 ounces) refrigerated French bread

6 thin slices deli ham

6 thin slices deli turkey breast

6 bacon strips, cooked and crumbled

1 tomato, seeded and diced

2 tablespoons scallions, chopped

1 cup shredded cheddar cheese

1/4 cup prepared ranch dressing

2 tablespoons butter, melted

1 teaspoon dried Italian seasoning or dried parsley

Unroll dough on baking sheet that has been sprayed with cooking spray. Roll out into a large rectangle. Spread with Ranch dressing, leaving about 2 inches on each side. Layer on ham, turkey, bacon, scallions and tomatoes. Top with cheese. Roll up the dough and press to seal the end seams.   Brush with butter and sprinkle with Italian seasoning or parsley. Bake at 350 degrees for 25 to 30 minutes. Cut into 2 inch slices and serve warm.

෨ ෨ ෨

It's still one of my all time favorite sandwiches- "The Club"! Turkey, ham, and bacon, I mean you can't go wrong with that! This is a fun take on the old classic. Great for a ladies lunch or family brunch too! I like to serve it with a fresh fruit salad on the side. (No, I don't usually cut up all that fruit! That's what grocery stores are for!)

෨ ෨ ෨

Cheesy Chicken and Broccoli Pockets

2 packages (8 ounces) refrigerated crescent rolls

1/4 cup finely chopped red pepper

1 cup frozen chopped broccoli, thawed and patted dry

1/4 cup water chestnuts, drained and chopped

2 tablespoons chopped scallions

1 cup shredded cheddar cheese

2 cups cooked chicken, finely chopped

1/4 to 1/3 cup mayonnaise

1 tablespoon lemon juice

1/4 teaspoon garlic salt

1/4 teaspoon black pepper

2 tablespoons of melted butter

2 tablespoons seasoned dry Italian bread crumbs

In a large bowl mix together mayonnaise, lemon juice, garlic salt and pepper. Mix in red pepper, broccoli, water chestnuts, scallions, cheese and chicken. Open the cans of crescent rolls. Don't separate the dough into triangles. Instead, keep two triangles together and separate the dough into 8 big squares. Press together the seams. Spoon a quarter of the chicken mixture in the center of the 4 squares of dough. Place the remaining 4 squares of dough on top. Seal up the dough with a fork. Brush each pocket with butter and sprinkle with bread crumbs. Bake on a cookie sheet in a preheated 350 degree oven for 15 to 25 minutes or until golden brown. Serve right away. Makes 4 pockets.

Baked Reuben Roll

1/2 package (17.5 ounces) frozen puff pastry (1 sheet) thawed

3 tablespoons Dijon mustard

1/2 pound corned beef, thinly sliced or finely chopped

1½ cups shredded Swiss cheese

1 cup sauerkraut, drained well

1 egg, beaten

1 tablespoon poppy seeds (optional)

Thousand Island dressing (optional)

Preheat oven to 375 degrees. Roll out the pastry sheet a bit to form one big rectangle. Spread mustard over the pastry. Lay the corned beef, sauerkraut, and cheese on top of the pastry. Roll up the pastry jellyroll fashion. Tuck the ends under and press to seal. Brush the beaten egg all over and sprinkle with poppy seeds. Bake for 25 to 40 minutes or until golden. Cut into 2 or 3 inch pieces and serve with thousand island dressing for dipping.

∾ ∾ ∾

I LOVE a good reuben! This is a fun one! Another great way to use up leftover corned beef! And, we always seem to have a lot of it after St. Paddy's day. We love our sauerkraut in Wisconsin! In fact just about all of the country's kraut comes from a little place not too far from Green Bay. I've watched them make it. Too cool! Think, I might have smelled like kraut for a couple days after, but it was worth it!

∾ ∾ ∾

Brie, Ham and Pear Sandwich

4 slices of sourdough or firm white bread

1 tablespoon fig or apricot jam

2 tablespoon mayonnaise

6 thin slices deli ham

1 firm, but ripe pear cut into 6 slices

6 slices of brie cheese

A few tablespoons butter, softened

In a small bowl, mix together jam and mayonnaise. Preheat a panini maker, grill pan, skillet, or griddle. Place 2 slices of bread on work surface and spread half of the mayonnaise mixture on each slice. Divide ham between 2 sandwiches and arrange on top. Add a few slices of pear and then top the pears with slices of cheese. Place a slice of bread on top and spread some butter on it. Place the sandwiches buttered side down in the pan. Then butter the top side. Grill until nicely browned on one side and then flip and grill other side. Cut each sandwich in half and serve right away.

∾ ∾ ∾

This is a grown-up grilled cheese recipe, but I think the kids will like it too. I bought the kids a panini maker a couple years ago, and they LOVE it! They make their own paninis now all the time. Get those kids in the kitchen!!! Do what ever it takes to get them in there! As you can see, I started early.

∾ ∾ ∾

By the way instead of pear, apples slices would work great in this sandwich. You could use apple butter instead of the fig or apricot jam. Not a big brie fan, have you ever tried it? It's really creamy and good! Don't be scared of the fancy name! But, you could use sliced cheddar, muenster or havarti instead. Just a fun way to jazz up an ordinary grilled cheese! This sandwich with the Tomato Basil Bisque in the "Soup's On" chapter makes one delicious dinner!!

Riley, age 6, and Ireland, age 1, helping out in the kitchen. As you can see, I started early. I always let the kids help when I was making a dessert. I let them measure, crack eggs, and yes, even lick the beaters once in awhile. Whatever it takes to get them interested in cooking. It's working! Ireland cooks all the time and Riley even made us dinner one night. Hopefully he'll do it again soon!

Grilled Buffalo Chicken Sandwiches

4 boneless, skinless chicken breast halves

Salt and pepper

2 tablespoons of olive oil

1 cup hot sauce (I like Frank's for this)

1 stick butter

2 cups sour cream

1 cup mayonnaise

4 ounces bleu cheese, crumbled

1 tablespoon lemon juice

2 tablespoons fresh chopped Italian parsley

4 hard or hoagie rolls, spilt and toasted

4 pieces of leaf lettuce

2 to 3 stalks celery, sliced

Season chicken with salt and pepper. Drizzle chicken with a little olive oil and grill or fry in a pan. While the chicken is grilling, melt butter and hot sauce together. Start brushing chicken with the hot sauce mixture. In a bowl, mix together sour cream, mayo, lemon juice, parsley, and bleu cheese. When chicken is done, dip in hot sauce so it's completely coated. To assemble sandwiches, spread bleu cheese mixture on both sides of the rolls. Next, on the bottom half of the roll, place a piece of lettuce and some celery. Put one chicken breast on each roll and put the top half of the bun on top. Extra bleu cheese mixture can be used to dip sandwich in or use as a dip for raw veggies.

KICKED UP CASSEROLES

Don't be scared, these are REALLY good

ones from the Queen of Casseroles!

My Secrets for a Seriously Good Casserole

Okay, okay, I get it! Casseroles get a really bad rap. We've all had that not so great one! You remember! It was dry or boring, or maybe it was even scary! Like, "what in the world is in that" scary?

I call myself the "Queen of Casseroles." I guess I always wanted to be the queen of something! Anyway, casseroles can be a real life saver! No time to make dinner, pull that casserole out of the fridge or freezer and throw it in the oven. Most casseroles freeze great! You just have to cover them really well!! I usually wrap them first in plastic and then foil on top too. On my big "Cooking Day", I usually make a couple casseroles. One for now and one to freeze for later.

Casseroles are also great when you're having company over. YES, you can serve a casserole at a dinner party- if it's a really good one! The best part, you can make them ahead of time. That way you're not stuck in the kitchen while everybody else is out there having a great time. HATE THAT! Just make sure to always spray that casserole dish with cooking spray! And, I mean ALWAYS!! Or else, after the party you'll be up half the night trying to get that dish cleaned. DEFINITELY HATE THAT!

Casseroles go wrong when you throw everything but the kitchen sink in there and toss in a can of cream of whatever soup. You need to think about everything you put in a casserole. Is it all going to work together? It needs to! You'll notice my casseroles have a lot of liquid in them. That makes them nice and creamy and not dry. NOBODY LIKES A DRY CASSEROLE! Remember pasta, rice, and potatoes soak that liquid right up! I use wine (not the real expensive stuff) in many of my recipes because it adds so much flavor. You can always use stock instead. Bottom line, make sure to use enough liquid.

My casseroles usually have cheese –IN- them and –ON- top. Hey, I live in Wisconsin! The more cheese the better. Have fun with the cheese, change it up and use different kinds!

And, you've gotta have some crunchies on top. From bread crumbs, to potato chips, to cornflakes and even pretzels. Love that crunchy top! It's the best part. Of yeah, and don't forget to put a little butter on top too! Now, that's a good casserole.

Now, every oven is different. So don't always go by my bake times. You know when that casserole's ready. When it's bubbly, golden on top and you're starting to drool! Toss together a salad, and pick up dessert (or make one of mine if you have the time) and that's why I LOVE, LOVE, LOVE my casseroles. It's dinner made easy, and really good too!

Chicken Cordon Bleu Bake

6 boneless, skinless chicken breast halves

Salt and pepper

1/4 pound shaved deli ham

6 slices Swiss cheese

2 cans (10.75 ounces) cream of chicken soup

2¼ cups milk

1 cup sour cream

1/4 cup dry white wine or chicken stock

1 stick butter, melted

2 boxes (6 ounces) chicken stuffing mix

Preheat oven to 325 degrees. Spray a 9" × 13" baking dish with cooking spray. Place chicken on the bottom. Season chicken with salt and pepper. Top each chicken breast with a few slices of ham and 1 slice of cheese. In a bowl, whisk together cream of chicken soup with milk, wine and sour cream and pour over chicken. Sprinkle dry stuffing mix on top of chicken. Drizzle butter over the top. Cover with foil and baked for about 1 hour. Remove foil and bake another 15 to 30 minutes.

~ ~ ~

This is one of those recipes everybody asks me for. It's so good and so easy. Serve it with a salad and maybe some rolls (no, I don't make homemade rolls, we're talking a tube of crescent rolls) and dinner is done! Rock star status, once again!

~ ~ ~

Smothered Chicken Casserole

6 boneless, skinless chicken breast halves

Salt and pepper

1 jar (1.5 ounces) sliced dried beef

6 strips of bacon

2 cups sour cream

2 cans (10.75 ounces) mushroom soup

2 cups milk

1/4 cup dry white wine or chicken stock

1/4 cup sliced almonds (optional)

Season chicken breasts with a little salt and pepper. Wrap each piece of chicken in a strip of bacon and then top with a few slices of dried beef and place in a 9" × 13" pan that has been sprayed with cooking spray. In a big bowl, whisk together mushroom soup with sour cream, milk, and wine. Pour over top of chicken. Cover with foil and bake at 325 degrees for about an hour. Uncover and sprinkle almonds on top if you want. Bake another 10 to 20 minutes longer. Great with hot cooked rice or mashed potatoes.

෨ ෨ ෨

Okay, I think this is why Bob married me. Seriously!! This is "the" very first dinner I ever made for him when we were dating in college. One bite and he was hooked! He's a "chicken guy!" Loves chicken and he loves casseroles too. Thank goodness or else I'd be in trouble, cause that's what I do! We love this with wild rice, just the wild rice blend in the box, don't have time usually to make the other kind!

෨ ෨ ෨

❧ ❧ ❧

I talk about him all the time. Well, here's my guy, Bob! He and Ireland love to fly. They both want to fly their own plane one day. Until then they just go up with other pilots we know. Here they are at the Harbor Springs, Michigan airport. I was at home cooking and worrying the whole time!

❧ ❧ ❧

Cheesy Chicken Spaghetti Casserole

1 package (16 ounces) spaghetti noodles, cooked al dente

3 to 4 chicken boneless chicken breast halves, cooked and diced into bite size pieces

1 cup onion, finely diced

1 bell pepper, finely diced

1 cup celery, finely diced

3 tablespoons butter

1 teaspoon garlic salt

1/2 teaspoon black pepper

1 can (10.75 ounces) cream of chicken soup

1 can (10.75 ounces) cream of celery soup

2½ cups milk

1 cup chicken stock

1 box (16 ounces) processed cheese, cut in cubes

3 cups shredded cheddar cheese

1/2 cup seasoned Italian bread crumbs

Preheat oven to 350 degrees. In a large soup pan, melt butter. Add onion, bell pepper, celery. Season with garlic salt and pepper and cook on medium low heat until vegetables are soft. Add both soups, milk, stock and processed cheese. Cook stirring constantly until cheese melts. Then, add chicken and spaghetti. Mix will. Pour spaghetti mixture into a 9" x 13" baking dish that has been sprayed with cooking spray. Sprinkle cheddar cheese and then bread crumbs on top. Bake covered loosely with foil for 30 to 45 minutes. Uncover and bake for another 10 or 15 minutes until bubbly and the bread crumbs are golden.

$\backsim$ $\backsim$ $\backsim$

This is another one of my most popular recipes. Kids love it! Grown ups love it! Everybody just LOVES it! Wish I could take the credit for this one but I actually got this recipe from the wife of former Green Bay Packer, Doug Pederson. What a sweetie! This is the casserole she brings over to new moms. She told me one player was up in the middle of the night with a crying baby, got hungry and ate this casserole cold right out of the fridge. It's THAT good!! But, I'd heat it up! Thanks Jeannie! Every time I make this people go crazy over it! Why not double the recipe and make two, one for your family and another one for somebody you know who just had a new baby or could use a little extra help with dinner. Great with some warm rolls and the Strawberry Salad recipe in the "Super Salads" chapter.

$\backsim$ $\backsim$ $\backsim$

Chicken Noodle Casserole

6 tablespoons butter, divided

1 cup onion, finely diced

1 cup celery, finely diced

1/2 teaspoon garlic salt

Salt and pepper

2 cans (10.75 ounces) cream of chicken soup

1 jar (2 ounces) pimentos, drained (optional)

2 cups milk

2 cups sour cream

1/4 cup dry white wine or chicken stock

2 to 3 cups cubed cooked chicken breast

1 bag (16 ounces) egg noodles, boiled and drained (slightly undercook them)

1/2 cup seasoned Italian bread crumbs

1/4 cup grated Parmesan cheese

In a skillet, melt 3 tablespoons butter. Sauté onions and celery in butter on medium heat until they start to get soft. Season with a little salt and pepper. In a large bowl whisk together soup, milk, wine, sour cream, garlic salt and a little black pepper. Mix until smooth. Add chicken, pimento, cooked vegetables and noodles. Pour into 9" × 13" baking dish that has been sprayed with cooking spray. Sprinkle bread crumbs on top of noodles. Next, sprinkle Parmesan cheese on top of bread crumbs. Melt remaining 3 tablespoons of butter and drizzle on top, Cover loosely with foil and bake in a preheated 350 degree oven for 25 to 35 minutes. Uncover and bake another 10 to 20 minutes until brown and bubbly.

$\backsim\ \backsim\ \backsim$

I think of my mom whenever I make this. She's a huge fan of chicken and noodles! My mom doesn't do fast food of any kind, never has! On our annual road trip every summer from Arizona to our cottage in northern Michigan finding a place for mom to eat along the way was, let's say, always a treasure hunt. My poor dad would get on the CB radio (remember those?) and ask truckers if there was any good, home cookin' around. Sure enough, we'd find some. They never were fancy but the food was always (well, pretty much always) fantastic! If it was on the menu, mom always ordered, and still does, the homemade chicken noodle soup. Love you mom! And dad too! How many guys would have driven all over kingdom come looking for chicken and noodles?

$\backsim\ \backsim\ \backsim$

Divine Chicken Divan

4 chicken breasts, cooked and pulled into pieces (no bones of course!)

1 bag (16 ounces) frozen broccoli, thawed

2 cans (10.75 ounces) cream of chicken soup

1 cup mayonnaise

1 cup sour cream

1½ cups milk

1 tablespoon fresh lemon juice

1 teaspoon curry powder

1/2 teaspoon black pepper

1/2 cup dry white wine

3 cups shredded sharp cheddar cheese

2 cups crushed garlic croutons

Preheat oven to 350 degrees. In a big bowl whisk together the soup, mayonnaise, sour cream, milk, lemon juice, curry powder, wine and pepper. Mix in broccoli and chicken. Spoon into casserole dish that has been sprayed with cooking spray. Top with cheddar cheese and croutons. Bake covered for 25 to 40 minutes. Uncover and bake another 10 to 20 minutes until croutons are slightly toasted. Great served with hot buttered white rice.

∞ ∞ ∞

My mom and dad went to dinner at a friend's, and when she got home all she could talk about was this casserole. We got the recipe and we've been making it ever since. Serve it with a salad and rolls and it's a winner! Great way to use up leftover chicken. You can use turkey too!

∞ ∞ ∞

Chicken and Wild Rice Casserole

1 box (6 ounces) long grain and wild rice blend

3 tablespoons butter

1 cup onion, finely diced

1 cup celery, finely diced

1 teaspoon garlic salt

1/2 teaspoon black pepper

1½ cups chicken stock

1/4 cup water

1/4 cup dry white wine (optional)

2 cups asparagus cut in 1inch pieces

3 cups shredded or cubed cooked chicken

1 can (8 ounces) sliced water chestnuts, drained

1 can (10.75 ounces) condensed cream of celery soup

1 can (10. 75 ounces) condensed cream of chicken soup

1 cup mayonnaise

1 cup milk

2 teaspoons lemon juice

3 cups shredded Swiss cheese

1/2 cup sliced almonds

Prepare wild rice according to package, less 1/4 cup water. In a large skillet, melt butter. Sauté onion and celery for a few minutes. Season with garlic salt and pepper. Add chicken stock, water and wine. Bring to a boil and add asparagus. Cook asparagus for a few minutes until it just starts to get tender. In a large bowl, whisk together both soups, milk, mayonnaise, and lemon juice. Stir in rice, chicken, water chestnuts and vegetable mixture with liquid. Mix well. Spoon into a 9" × 13" baking dish that has been sprayed with cooking spray.   Sprinkle with cheese and then almonds. Baked covered in foil in a preheated 350 over for 40 to 50 minutes. Uncover and bake another 15 to 25 minutes until bubbly and nuts are a little brown.

෴ ෴ ෴

I was so excited when I came up with this recipe. When March rolls around, I start getting real tired of winter and absolutely crave all things spring, like asparagus! So, this is what I call my "Spring Casserole". It's usually still pretty cold and snowy when spring rolls around in Wisconsin, so I'm not ready to quit eating casseroles quite yet. Still need my warm, comfort food, so this dish is my little taste of spring.

෴ ෴ ෴

Warm Chicken Salad Casserole

6 skinless, boneless chicken breast halves, cooked and shredded or finely diced

2 cups chopped celery

1/4 cup onion, finely diced

2 cups mayonnaise

1/2 cup milk

1 can (10.75 ounces) condensed cream of chicken soup

1 jar (2 ounces) diced pimentos, drained

2 tablespoons fresh lemon juice

1/4 cup dry white wine or chicken stock

1 teaspoon garlic salt

1/2 teaspoon black pepper

3 cups shredded sharp cheddar cheese

2 cups crushed potato chips

2/3 cup slivered or sliced almonds

In a large bowl whisk together mayonnaise, milk, wine or stock, soup, lemon juice, garlic salt and pepper. Stir in chicken, celery, onion, and pimentos. Mix well and spoon into a 9" x 13" baking dish that's been sprayed with cooking spray. Sprinkle cheese, potato chips and almonds on top, in that order. Bake uncovered in a preheated 350 degree oven for 30 to 45 minutes until hot and bubbly.

Terrific Tetrazzini

1 box (16 ounces) spaghetti, cooked al dente

1 cup celery, finely diced

1 cup onion, finely diced

1/2 cup green pepper, finely diced

8 ounces sliced mushrooms

1 teaspoon garlic salt

1/2 teaspoon black pepper

8 tablespoons (1 stick) butter, divided

2 cans (10.75 ounces) cream of mushroom or cream of chicken soup

2 cups sour cream

2¼ cups milk

1/4 cup sherry or dry white wine

3 to 4 cups shredded or diced cooked turkey or chicken

1/2 cup seasoned Italian bread crumbs

1/2 cup grated parmesan cheesc

In a large skillet, heat 3 tablespoons of butter. Cook celery, green pepper and onion in butter for a few minutes. Add another two tablespoons of butter and the mushrooms and cook for another couple minutes until the veggies start to get soft. Season with garlic salt and pepper. In a large bowl, whisk together milk, soup, sour cream and sherry or wine. Add pasta, chicken or turkey and vegetables. Mix well. Spoon into a 9" × 13" pan that has been sprayed with cooking spray. Sprinkle the top with bread crumbs. Next, sprinkle parmesan cheese on top. Melt the remaining 3 tablespoons of butter and drizzle it over the top .Bake loosely covered with foil in a preheated 350 degree oven for 25 to 40 minutes. Uncover and bake another 15 to 20 minutes or until hot, golden and bubbly.

Turkey and Stuffing Casserole

3 to 4 cups sliced or cubed cooked turkey

2 cans (10.75 ounces) cream of mushroom soup

2 cups sour cream

2 cups milk

1/4 cup dry white wine or chicken stock

1/2 teaspoon black pepper

1/2 teaspoon garlic salt

1 teaspoon dried tarragon or parsley

2 boxes (6 ounces) chicken or turkey flavored stuffing mix (prepared according to directions)

3 tablespoons melted butter

In a large bowl, mix together sour cream, mushroom soup, milk, wine, and seasonings. Mix turkey or chicken in with soup mixture. Spray a 9" × 13" pan with cooking spray. Spoon in the turkey mixture. Top with prepared stuffing. Drizzle butter on top. Bake covered in foil in a preheated 350 degree oven for 35 to 45 minutes. Uncover and bake another 10 to 20 minutes or until it's bubbly and the stuffing gets a little browned.

❧ ❧ ❧

Okay, when you are craving Thanksgiving dinner, make this casserole. It's a lot less work! Sometimes I'll roast or grill a turkey breast and use the leftovers to make this. This recipe works great with leftover chicken too!

❧ ❧ ❧

Beer and Cheese Mac n' Cheese

6 tablespoons butter

1/2 cup finely diced onion

2 cloves garlic, minced

3 tablespoons flour

1 teaspoon garlic salt

1/4 teaspoon black pepper

1 tablespoon Dijon mustard

1 bottle (12 ounces) beer

2½ cups milk

5 cups shredded sharp cheddar cheese

A few dashes hot sauce

1 box (16 ounces) elbow macaroni, cooked al dente

8 pieces bacon, cooked and crumbled

1/4 cup grated parmesan cheese

1 cup finely crushed sourdough pretzels

Melt butter in a large non-stick pan. Cook onion in butter over medium heat until soft. Add garlic and cook another 30 seconds. Whisk in flour stirring for a minute or two until well combined. Add beer and milk, whisking constantly. Bring to a boil. When it starts to thicken, turn down heat. Add mustard, garlic salt, pepper and 3 cups of cheese, a handful at a time. Whisk until cheese is melted. Add hot sauce. Remove from heat and stir in macaroni and bacon. Spoon into a 9" × 13" casserole dish that has been sprayed with cooking spray. Top with remaining 2 cups of cheddar cheese and then parmesan cheese and pretzels. Bake in a preheated 350 degree oven for 35 to 45 minutes until bubbly.

The Kids (and my) Favorite Tator Tot Casserole

2 pounds ground beef

1 teaspoon garlic salt

1/2 teaspoon freshly ground black pepper

2 cans (10 ounces) cream of mushroom soup

1 cup sour cream

1½ cups milk

1 can (14.5 ounces) French green beans, drained

1½ cups corn

3 to 4 cups shredded cheddar cheese

1 package (32 ounces) frozen tator tots

1 to 2 teaspoons steak seasoning salt

Preheat oven to 350 degrees. Spray a 9" × 13" pan with cooking spray. Brown ground beef in a skillet. Drain any grease. Season beef with garlic salt and pepper. Place beef in the baking dish. Place beans and corn on top of beef. In a large bowl, whisk together soup, milk and sour cream. Spread over ground beef in an even layer. Top with tator tots. Sprinkle tots with seasoning salt. Top with cheese. Bake 30 to 40 minutes covered loosely with foil. Uncover and bake another 10 to 15 minutes until cheese is bubbly.

∽ ∽ ∽

Okay, this really is one of my favorite casseroles. I know, it's not very fancy, but what the heck, it's really good!

∽ ∽ ∽

Reuben Casserole

1 loaf rye bread, cut into cubes

1/2 cup or 1 stick of butter

1 pound bag (16 ounces) sauerkraut, drained

3 cups shredded Swiss cheese

1½ cups of sour cream

1 cup Thousand Island dressing

2 to 3 cups corned beef, diced

2 teaspoons caraway seeds (optional)

2 tablespoons of fresh chopped Italian parsley or 1 tablespoon of dried parsley

Heat the butter in a large skillet. Add the bread cubes. Cook the bread crumbs for a few minutes so they toast up a bit. Put half of the bread cubes into a 9" × 13" pan that has been sprayed with cooking spray. Spoon the sauerkraut on top of the bread cubes. Sprinkle caraway seeds on top. Mix the sour cream and Thousand Island dressing together and spoon half of it on top of sauerkraut. Top with 1 cup of Swiss cheese, then the corned beef. Then spoon on the rest of the sour cream mixture and lastly the rest of the bread cubes and 2 cups of Swiss cheese. Sprinkle parsley on top. Cover with foil and bake at 350 degrees for 25 to 35 minutes. Uncover and bake an extra 10 minutes.

∞ ∞ ∞

Yum, Yum., Yum! Got leftover corned beef. We usually have tons of it after St, Paddy's Day! Freeze it. Then, when you're craving corned beef make this casserole. It's so good! No leftover corned beef, just go to the deli and get some. You'll be glad you did! Thanks Sarah for this one too!

∞ ∞ ∞

Gorgonzola Pasta Bake with Italian Sausage

1 box (16 ounces) penne pasta, cooked al dente

1 pound sweet Italian sausage, cooked, crumbled and cooled

2½ cups heavy cream

1/4 cup chicken stock

2 tablespoons dry white wine

Fresh ground black pepper

1 can (14 ounces) diced tomatoes, drained

3/4 cup freshly grated parmesan cheese, divided

1½ cups gorgonzola cheese, crumbled

2 teaspoons dried basil

1½ cups garlic croutons, crushed

3 tablespoons butter

In a large sauce pan, heat the cream, stock and wine. Simmer for a few minutes. Stir in gorgonzola and half cup of parmesan cheese. Whisk until smooth. Season sauce with a little black pepper. In a large bowl, toss sauce with pasta, sausage, tomatoes and basil. Pour into large casserole dish that has been sprayed with cooking spray. Top with croutons and remaining parmesan. Dot butter over the top in small pieces. Cover loosely with foil and bake in preheated 350 degree oven for 25 to 40 minutes minutes. Uncover and bake another 8 to 15 minutes until top is slightly browned.

〜 〜 〜

Okay, hate to brag but this casserole is AMAZING!! Even people who don't really do bleu cheese love it. The heavy cream and parmesan really mellow it out. It's fancy enough for company or even for a dinner party. The best part, it's a casserole! So you can make it ahead of time and bake it right before dinner. Serve it with a big salad and bread and talk about "rock star"! You are one! And. hey you can substitute 2 cups diced, cooked chicken breasts in place of the Italian sausage or make it with no meat at all. Just make this one! Seriously!

〜 〜 〜

Baked Ravioli Casserole

1 pound ground beef

2 teaspoons garlic salt

1 bag (24 ounces) frozen cheese ravioli, slightly thawed

3 to 4 cups shredded mozzarella cheese

1/4 cup grated parmesan cheese

1 jar (24 to 28 ounces) marinara sauce

1¼ cups water

1½ cups crushed garlic croutons

3 tablespoons melted butter

In a big skillet brown ground beef over medium-high heat until crumbly and no longer pink. Season beef with garlic salt. Add sauce and water. Simmer for a couple minutes. Spread a small amount of the meat sauce in the bottom of a 9" x 13" casserole dish that's been sprayed with cooking spray. Spread half of the ravioli in bottom of the dish. Spoon some of the sauce over the ravioli. Next sprinkle half of the mozzarella cheese over the sauce. Now, it's time for the rest of the ravioli, the rest of the sauce and the rest of the mozzarella. Sprinkle the Parmesan cheese and then the croutons on top. Drizzle butter over the top. Bake in preheated 350 degree oven for 25 to 35 minutes.

∾ ∾ ∾

This is a super quick fix! We're talking less then ten minutes to throw this together. It's like lasagna but way easier to make! My kids love this with garlic bread. Hey, teach your kids to make this one! Then, they can start helping make dinner every once in awhile. Now, wouldn't that be nice???

∾ ∾ ∾

Super Easy Baked Ziti

1 box (16 ounces) ziti, cooked al dente

1 pound ground beef or Italian sausage, casings removed

1/2 cup onion, chopped

3 teaspoons garlic salt

1 jar (24 to 28 ounces) marinara sauce

1¼ cups water

1/4 cup white wine (optional)

3 to 4 cups mozzarella cheese

2 tablespoons grated parmesan cheese

1 cup crushed garlic croutons

Cook ground beef or sausage and chopped onions in a skillet over medium heat until crumbly and no longer pink. Season with garlic salt. Add sauce, wine and water. Simmer a couple minutes. Toss sauce and pasta together. Spoon into a 9" × 13" casserole dish that's been sprayed with cooking spray. Top with mozzarella, then Parmesan and croutons. Bake at 350 for 20 to 35 minutes until bubbly.

∾ ∾ ∾

Here's another easy one! Great for those picky eaters who we all know and love! Nothing "scary" in this casserole so it's super kid friendly. Garlic bread and a salad and you've got one happy family!

∾ ∾ ∾

Spinach Lasagna Roll Ups

12 lasagna noodles, cooked al dente

2 eggs, lightly beaten

1 packet (.5 ounce) dry pesto sauce mix

1 container (15 ounces) ricotta cheese

4 cups shredded mozzarella cheese, divided

1/4 cup grated parmesan cheese, divided

1 package (10 ounces) frozen chopped spinach, thawed and squeezed dry

1 pound ground beef

1 cup onion, finely diced

1 teaspoon garlic salt

1/2 teaspoon black pepper

1 jar (24 to 28 ounces) marinara sauce

1 can (28 ounces) crushed tomatoes with juice

1/4 cup dry white or red wine (optional)

Brown beef with onion until crumbly and no longer pink. Season with garlic salt and pepper. Add tomatoes, spaghetti sauce, and wine. Bring to a boil, turn down heat and let simmer for 10 to 15 minutes until sauce thickens a bit. In a bowl combine eggs, spinach, 1 cup mozzarella cheese, parmesan cheese and pesto package. Spread 1/3 cup cheese mixture over each noodle, carefully roll up. Then, sprinkle the rest of the mozzarella cheese on top. Pour some of the meat sauce into a 9" × 13" baking dish that's been sprayed with cooking spray. Place roll ups seam side down over sauce. Spoon some of the remaining sauce over each roll up. Bake loosely covered with foil at 375 degrees for 20 to 30 minutes, uncover and bake another 5 to 10 minutes until bubbly.

Shepherd's Pie

2 pounds ground round beef

1 cup onion, finely diced

1 cup celery, finely diced

1 teaspoon garlic salt

1/2 teaspoon black pepper

4 tablespoons flour

1 bag (16 ounces) assorted frozen vegetables, slightly thawed (carrots, corn, peas, green beans)

4 to 5 cups beef stock

2 teaspoons Worcestershire sauce

1 can (10.75 ounces) cream on mushroom soup

6 to 8 potatoes, peeled and boiled

1/4 cup warm milk

1/4 cup grated parmesan cheese

3 tablespoons butter, melted

In a large skillet, brown beef with onion and celery until beef is crumbly and no longer pink. Season with garlic salt and pepper. Stir in flour. Cook a minute or two. Add Worcestershire sauce and 4 cups of beef stock and bring to a simmer until the sauce starts to thicken a bit. Stir in mushroom soup and vegetables. If gravy seems a little thick add some extra stock. Spoon mixture into a large casserole dish that has been sprayed with cooking spray. In a bowl mash potatoes with some milk until they are smooth. Mix in the parmesan cheese. Spread mashed potatoes on top of the beef and vegetables,   Drizzle butter over the top. Bake in a preheated, 375 degree oven for 30 to 45 minutes until bubbly and the potatoes are a little golden. You can use the broiler if you need to brown the top a bit.

Terrific Tuna Casserole

2 tablespoons butter

1 cup onion, finely diced

1 cup celery, finely diced

1 teaspoon garlic salt

2 cans (10.75 ounces) cream of mushroom soup

1¾ cups milk

1/4 cup dry white wine (optional)

1 cup frozen peas, slightly thawed

2 cans (5 ounces) albacore tuna packed in water, drained

3 cups shredded cheddar cheese

2 cups crushed potato chips

1 bag (16 ounces) egg noodles, cooked al dente

Preheat oven to 350 degrees. In a large pan melt the butter. Cook onion and celery in the butter until the vegetables start to get soft. Season with garlic salt and pepper. Add mushroom soup, milk, and wine. Stir and heat until smooth. Add tuna, noodles and peas. Stir and coat with the sauce. Spoon into a 9" × 13" inch baking dish that has been sprayed with cooking spray and top with cheese and potato chips. Bake for 35 to 55 minutes until bubbly and chips are golden.

Blend of the Bayou Seafood Casserole

1 package (8 ounces) cream cheese, cut into small cubes

4 tablespoons of butter

1 cup onion, finely diced

1 green pepper, finely diced

2 stalks celery, finely diced

1/2 teaspoon garlic salt

1 teaspoon Old Bay seafood seasoning

1/2 teaspoon Cajun seasoning

1 can (10.75 ounces) cream of mushroom soup

1½ cups milk

dash of hot sauce

1 pound peeled and cooked shrimp

1 can (4.25 ounces) crab meat, drained

8 ounces sliced mushrooms

1½ to 2 cups cooked white rice

3 cups shredded cheddar cheese

2 cups crushed butter flavored crackers

Sauté peppers, onion, and celery in 3 tablespoons of butter for a few minutes. Add mushrooms and cook another few minutes until they just start to get soft. Season with garlic salt, cajun seasoning and Old Bay. Add cream of mushroom soup, cream cheese, milk and hot sauce. Heat until smooth; stirring often. Stir in shrimp, crab meat, and rice. Spoon into a casserole dish that has been sprayed with cooking spray. Top with cheese and crushed crackers. Bake in a preheated 350 degree oven for 30 to 45 minutes until brown and bubbly. Serve it with a little extra hot sauce if you can stand the heat.

Easy Chicken Enchiladas

1 handful of fresh cilantro

1 cup sour cream

1/2 cup chicken stock

1 jar (16 ounces) salsa (green or red)

1 can (4 ounces) diced green chilies

1 teaspoon cumin

3 cups cooked and shredded chicken

8 (6 to 8") flour tortillas

2 to 3 cups shredded Mexican blend or monterey jack cheese

Extra sour cream, black olives, scallions, cilantro

Put first four ingredients in a blender and blend for just a second. Sauce should still be a little chunky. In a large bowl, combine shredded chicken, cumin and green chilies. Preheat oven to 350 degrees. Heat tortillas in the microwave (a few at a time) for a few seconds until soft. Pour a little of the sauce mixture into a 9" x 13" baking dish, that's been sprayed with cooking spray. Place some of the chicken mixture in each tortilla, roll up and place seam side down in the baking dish. Pour remaining sauce over the enchiladas and top with shredded cheese. Cover dish loosely with foil and bake for about 20 to 30 minutes, uncover and bake another 10 to 15 minutes or until bubbly. Serve with "extras" on top if you want. (And, I do!! Please pass the sour cream!!)

Green Chili Pork Enchiladas

2 cups shredded, cooked pork

1 can (10.75 ounces) cream of chicken soup

2 teaspoons ground cumin

1 can (4 ounces) diced green chilies

2 cups shredded monterey jack cheese

2 cups green salsa or green enchilada sauce

8 (6" size) corn tortillas

Sour cream

Fresh cilantro

Chopped scallions

In a small bowl, combine the shredded pork with green chilies, cumin and soup. In skillet, heat the salsa or enchilada sauce. Remove from heat. Dip each tortilla into the heated sauce to soften. Spoon some of the shredded pork mixture down the center of each tortilla. Roll and place each filled tortilla, seam side down into a 9" × 13" baking dish that has been sprayed with cooking spray. Pour remaining heated enchilada sauce over top and sprinkle the shredded cheese on top. Bake in a preheated 350 degree oven for 25 to 30 minutes until hot and bubbly. Serve with sour cream, scallions, and cilantro on top.

Shrimp Enchiladas

3 tablespoons olive oil

1/2 cup onion, finely diced

1/4 cup red pepper, finely diced

1 fresh jalapeno, finely diced (optional if you want a little heat)

1 teaspoon garlic salt

1/2 teaspoon chili powder

1/2 teaspoon cumin

1½ pounds peeled, deveined medium shrimp

Juice from half a small lime

1 container (8 ounces) chive and onion cream cheese

2 cups shredded monterey jack cheese

10 medium flour tortillas

1 jar (16 ounces) green or red salsa (I prefer the green in this one, but it's up to you)

1 cup heavy cream

Sauté onion and red pepper in oil in a large skillet. Stir in shrimp and jalapeno and season with garlic salt, cumin and chili powder. Cook shrimp it turns pink and squeeze lime juice over the top. Stir in cream cheese and heat until melted. Preheat oven to 350 degrees. In a bowl mix together heavy cream and salsa. Spoon some of the sauce into a 9" × 13" baking dish. Lay tortillas on a work surface and spoon some of the shrimp on top of each. Roll up and place, seam side down, into baking dish. Spoon remaining sauce over the top. Top with cheese and bake in a preheated 350 degree oven for 25 to 40 minutes until bubbly. Serve the enchiladas with sour cream and fresh cilantro if you like.

JUST THROW IT IN
THE SLOW COOKER

My new best friend and soon to be yours too!

Sloppy Joes for a Crowd

4 pounds lean ground beef

2 cups onion, finely diced

1½ cups celery, finely diced

1/2 cup green pepper, finely diced

Salt and pepper

4 cups ketchup

1 can (6 ounces) tomato paste

1/4 cup brown sugar

2 tablespoons worcestershire sauce

2 tablespoons apple cider vinegar

1/2 cup water

2 dozen buns

In large pan, brown ground beef with onions, celery and green pepper. Season with some salt and pepper. Drain off fat. Place ground beef in slowcooker, stir in ketchup, tomato paste, brown sugar, worcestershire, water and vinegar. Cover and cook on low for 4 to 5 hours, stirring occasionally. If too dry, add a little water. Serve on buns. Makes about 2 dozen sandwiches.

∾ ∾ ∾

Who says sloppy joes are just a "kid thing"? I love 'em!

∾ ∾ ∾

Hot Beef Sandwiches

4 pounds boneless beef roast (chuck or rump roast)

2 cans (10½ ounces) cream of mushroom soup

1 package dry onion soup mix

1½ cups beef stock

Buns or hard rolls (I like hard rolls fresh from the bakery!)

Put roast in the slow cooker. Mix the two cans of soup with stock and onion soup mix. Pour over the beef. Cover and cook on low for 8 to 10 hours or on high for 4 to 6 hours or until it's really tender. Use forks to shred the beef. If too thick add a little water. Serve warm on hard rolls.

෴ ෴ ෴

This is so easy and so good!! Throw it all in the slow cooker in the morning and head out and do your thing. Come home after work, and running those kids around to all their after school stuff, (sound familiar?) and the house smells AMAZING!! Once again you did it! Dinner is ready! Now, wasn't that easy! You'll probably have some leftovers too, so make sure and get a good size roast because I think leftovers are a good thing!

෴ ෴ ෴

Hot BBQ Beef Sandwiches

4 to 5 pounds boneless beef chuck roast

1 tablespoon garlic salt

2 teaspoons black pepper

2 tablespoons olive oil

1 onion sliced

1 bottle (16 to 18 ounces) of your favorite BBQ sauce (or whatever's on sale)

1/2 cup ketchup

1 can (12 ounces) of Coke (Not Diet!!! I don't like it anyway!)

Hamburger buns (about a dozen or more)

Extra BBQ sauce (if you want it)

Season roast with garlic salt and pepper. Heat oil in a skillet. Brown roast for a few minutes on both sides. Throw the roast, the onions and all the rest of it in a slow cooker and cook on low for 8 to 10 hours or if you're in a rush (they say you can never rush a good thing!) on high for 4 to 6 hours, until it's really tender and just falls apart. Take the beef out of the pot and shred it with forks. Then, throw it back in there with the sauce. (Most times I just shred it right in the slowcooker! Less cleanup!) Add a little water if needed or some extra BBQ sauce. You can serve extra BBQ sauce on the side too if you want. Serve on buns.

Hot Italian Beef Sandwiches

1 teaspoon of salt

1 teaspoon black pepper

1 teaspoon dried oregano

1 teaspoon dried basil

1 teaspoon onion salt

1 teaspoon dried parsley

1 teaspoon garlic powder

1 bay leaf

1 packet (.75 ounce) dry Italian style salad dressing mix

3 cups water

5 pound rump roast

A dozen or so crusty rolls

Dump the first 10 ingredients into a sauce pan. Stir well and bring to a boil for a minute or two. Place roast in the slow cooker and pour spice mixture over roast. Cover and cook on low for 8 to 12 hours or on high for 4 to 6 or until beef just falls apart. Remove bay leaf and shred meat in the drippings with forks. Serve on rolls. The extra sauce in the slow cooker is great for dipping!

∾ ∾ ∾

The nicest guy made this for me on my show! I've been making them at home ever since. Just so easy! One of those dump and go recipes! Thanks Charles!! LOVE IT!

∾ ∾ ∾

Yankee Pot Roast

4 pound boneless beef chuck roast

2 tablespoons olive oil

2 teaspoons garlic salt

1 teaspoon black pepper

6 to 8 medium sized potatoes, quartered

2 cups peeled baby carrots

4 stalks celery, cut into 2 inch pieces

2 large onions, quartered

2 cans (10.75 ounces) cream of mushroom soup

2 cups beef stock

1 cup water

2 tablespoons tomato paste

Whisk together soup, water, stock, and tomato paste in the slow cooker. In a large skillet heat the oil. Season the roast with garlic salt and pepper. Brown the roast for a few minutes on each side. Place roast in soup mixture in the slow cooker. Set slow cooker on low and let cook for 6 to 8 hours. You can also cook on high for 4 to 5 hours or until the roast gets really tender. Next add potatoes, carrots, celery and onions to the cooker. Lift roast so vegetables are submerged in liquid. Cook on high for 1 to 2 hours until roast and vegetables are nice and tender. Remove roast and vegetables to a platter. Serve the sauce over the roast and vegetables. If you want to thicken the sauce you can whisk together a tablespoon or two of flour with about a half cup cold water. Place the drippings in a pan with the flour and water mixture and bring to a boil, whisking often until it starts to thicken. Season gravy with salt and pepper if needed.

Italian Pot Roast

4 pound boneless beef chuck roast

Salt and pepper

2 tablespoons olive oil

1 cup dry red wine

1 cup water

1 cup beef stock

1 can (28 ounces) diced tomatoes, with juice

1 onion sliced

4 stalks celery, cut in chunks

1 packet (.75 ounce) dry Italian salad dressing mix

1 (16 ounces) package mushrooms

4 tablespoons butter

2 teaspoons garlic salt

In a large skillet heat oil. Season roast well with salt and pepper. Brown beef for a few minutes in hot oil on both sides. Remove beef to a plate. Add water, wine, and beef stock to pan. Bring to a boil, scraping up brown bits. Place roast along with stock mixture into the slowcooker. Add canned tomatoes, onion, celery and Italian seasoning mix. Cover and cook on low for 8 to 10 hours or on high for 4 to 6 hours, or until roast is fork tender. Just before serving, cook mushrooms in a skillet with butter. Season mushrooms with garlic salt. Serve mushrooms with the roast and vegetables. Roast is great with mashed potatoes or hot buttered rice.

Cajun Pot Roast

4 pounds boneless beef chuck roast

2 tablespoons cajun seasoning

1 large onion, cut in big chunks

4 stalks celery, cut in big chunks

1 green pepper, chopped

1 can (28 ounces) diced tomatoes

1½ cups beef stock

Few dashes of hot sauce (optional)

Sprinkle cajun seasoning over roast and rub to coat well. Place roast in a slowcooker. Dump in everything else. Cover and cook on low for 8 to 10 hours or on high for 4 to 6 hours until meat is tender. Great over buttered white rice or mashed potatoes.

∾ ∾ ∾

Want to spice up your weeknight? Make this! It's not too spicy unless you want it to be. I know you're in a hurry, but if you can throw this in my best friend (you know, the crock pot) in the morning, you'll be a hero at dinner time! And the house is going to smell so good!

∾ ∾ ∾

Easy Irish Beef Stew

2 to 3 pounds beef stew meat

1 envelope dry beefy onion soup mix

1/2 teaspoon black pepper

1 bottle (12 ounces) beer or 1 ½ cups water

A few dashes Worcestershire sauce

2 onions, cut in chunks

2 cups peeled baby carrots

4 stalks celery, cut in 2 inch chunks

1 can (28 ounces) diced tomatoes with juice

1 bay leaf

4 to 6 medium sized potatoes, cut in chunks

1/3 cup quick cooking tapioca

Place the beef in the slow cooker. Add the beefy onion soup mix and pepper and toss with the beef. Add the remaining ingredients and stir well. Cover and cook on low heat for 8 to 10 hours or on high for 4 to 6 hours. If stew gets too thick you can add some beef stock or water.

ন৺ ন৺ ন৺

There's nothing like a warm bowl of beef stew on a cold winter day! Throw this together in the morning before you go skiing or snowmobiling and you've got a wonderful dinner to come home to. No sides needed, it's all in there.

ন৺ ন৺ ন৺

Garlic Pork Roast

4 to 5 pound boneless pork butt roast

1 tablespoon garlic salt

2 teaspoons black pepper

2 tablespoons olive oil

1 medium yellow onion, sliced

4 to 6 cloves garlic, chopped

2 cups chicken stock

Trim excess fat from pork. Heat oil in a large skillet over medium-high heat. Season pork with garlic salt and pepper. Brown all sides of pork in oil for a few minutes. Place onion and garlic in a large crock pot. Place pork on top of onion and garlic. Pour stock over pork. Cover and cook on low heat setting 8-10 hours or on high for about 6 hours or until pork is tender. Shred pork with a fork. You can make a gravy with the drippings. Just take 2 tablespoons of flour and whisk it together with a half cup of cold water. Put it all in a sauce pan and boil it, whisking often until it gets thick. Taste it to see if it needs a little salt and pepper. Gotta serve this with mashed potatoes. See how to make perfect mashers in the "What's on the Side?" chapter.

ᘐ ᘐ ᘐ

Okay, here's a winner!!! You can take this one roast and make THREE, yes, THREE different meals out of it. Have it the traditional way with potatoes and gravy on the first night. On the second night you can shred the pork and toss it with BBQ sauce and serve it warm on buns. On the third night toss some shredded pork with a can of green chiles, wrap it in tortillas and make burritos.

ᘐ ᘐ ᘐ

Green Chili Pork Roast

4 to 5 pounds boneless pork butt roast

1 tablespoon garlic salt

3 teaspoons black pepper

2 tablespoons olive oil

3 cans (4 ounces) diced green chiles

2 cups chicken stock

Fresh lime juice

Trim the fat from the pork and season it with garlic salt and pepper. Heat oil in a large pan over medium high heat. Brown roast on both sides. Transfer the pork into the slow cooker. Pour green chilies and chicken stock over top. Cover and cook on low for 8 to 10 hours or on high for 5 to 6 hours. Shred pork with 2 forks in the slow cooker. If too dry, add a little more stock or some water. Squeeze a little fresh lime juice over pork before eating. Serve over hot buttered rice or in warm flour or corn tortillas with your favorite taco fixings.

ꙮ ꙮ ꙮ

My sister and her husband live in Arizona. They make shredded pork whenever I visit. I LOVE it! Especially when Sean deep frys the tortillas (come on Sean, do it!!) They've started to eat a little more healthy lately and I can't find their deep fryer. Sean makes "THE BEST" homemade tacos ever! Homemade fresh salsa too! Miss you guys! Got any leftovers, make my Pork Enchiladas in the "Kicked Up Casseroles" chapter or my Posole in the "Soup's On" chapter. And, one more thing, you can use a beef chuck roast instead of the pork and it works great too!

ꙮ ꙮ ꙮ

BBQ Pulled Pork Sandwiches

4 to 5 pound boneless pork butt roast

2 tablespoons garlic salt

1 tablespoon black pepper

1 can (10 ounces) Dr. Pepper (not diet)

1 sliced onion

1 bottle (16 ounces) of your favorite BBQ sauce

1½ cups ketchup

1/2 cup brown sugar

2 tablespoons Dijon mustard

Hamburger buns (a dozen or maybe more)

Trim any fat and season the roast with garlic salt and pepper. Place roast in a large slow cooker. Add onion and Dr. Pepper. Cover and cook for 8 to 10 hours on low or for 4 to 6 hours on high or until the roast is fork tender. About a half hour before you're ready to eat, heat BBQ sauce, brown sugar, ketchup and mustard together in a sauce pan. Stir well. Shred the pork with two forks. Add BBQ mixture sauce to the slow cooker. Mix with the shredded pork and heat for another 30 minutes or so. Serve on buns.

Apple Cranberry Pork Roast

3 to 4 pound boneless pork loin roast

2 cloves garlic, minced

Salt and pepper

1 can (16 ounces) whole berry cranberry sauce

1/4 cup brown sugar

3/4 cup apple juice

2 apples, peeled and chopped

Season roast with salt and pepper, and rub garlic all over it. Place roast in the slow cooker. Whisk together cranberry sauce, juice, and brown sugar. Pour it over the roast. Throw apples on top. Cover and cook on low for 6 to 8 hours or on high for 4 to 5 hours. It should be nice and tender! Slice and serve with the sauce. It's great with wild rice!

ᘒ ᘒ ᘒ

Cranberries, apples and pork! What's not to like? Another super easy recipe!! This is really nice in the fall! Light a fire in the fireplace, or a candle if you don't have one and get comfy!

ᘒ ᘒ ᘒ

Sante Fe Chicken

6 boneless skinless chicken breast halves

Salt and pepper

2 teaspoons ground cumin

1 jar (16 ounces) salsa

1 can (15 ounces) black beans, drained

1½ cups frozen corn

1/2 cup chicken stock

1 package (8 ounces) cream cheese

Shredded cheddar cheese (optional)

Fresh chopped cilantro (optional)

Fresh chopped scallions (optional)

Sour cream (optional)

Season chicken with salt, pepper, and cumin. Place in the slow cooker. Dump the salsa, beans, corn, and stock on top. Cover and cook on low for 6 to 8 hours or on high for 4 to 5 hours. Add the cream cheese and cook on high for another half hour or so until it melts. Serve with shredded cheddar cheese, scallions, cilantro and sour cream on top, if you want. Great with rice!

෨ ෨ ෨

Isn't this fun? It's Fiesta time! Start the night with my Tortilla Roll-ups or Guacamole (both recipes in the first chapter) and blend up some margaritas! It's going to be a great night!

෨ ෨ ෨

Italian Chicken in the Crockpot

2 cans cream of chicken soup

2 cloves minced garlic

1 teaspoon dried basil

1 teaspoon dried marjoram

1/4 teaspoon dried oregano

1/4 teaspoon onion powder

3/4 cup dry white wine (or you can use chicken stock)

1 cup milk

2 tablespoons drained capers

1 can (14 ounces) quartered artichoke hearts, drained

1/2 cup drained and chopped sun-dried tomatoes

6 boneless skinless chicken breast halves

Salt and pepper

1/2 cup chopped fresh basil leaves

Hot cooked pasta (we like it over buttered fettuccini)

In a bowl, whisk the first 8 ingredients together. Season the chicken with salt and pepper. Place chicken in the slow cooker. Pour soup mixture over the top. Stir to make sure all the chicken is coated. Cover and cook on low for 6 hours or on high for 3 to 4 hours. A half hour before serving throw in the capers, sun-dried tomatoes, and artichoke hearts. Cook on high for a half hour.   Sprinkle with fresh basil before serving.

French Dijon Chicken

1 large onion, cut in chunks

5 celery ribs, cut in chunks

2 cups peeled, baby carrots

6 boneless skinless chicken breast halves

Salt and pepper

1 tablespoon dried tarragon

1 teaspoon dried thyme

2 (10¾ ounce) cans condensed cream of chicken soup

4 tablespoons Dijon mustard

3/4 cup dry white wine or chicken stock

2 tablespoons chopped fresh tarragon or Italian parsley

Place onion, celery, and baby carrots in slow cooker. Season chicken with salt, pepper, tarragon and thyme. Place chicken over the vegetables. Whisk together soup, mustard and wine. Pour soup mixture over chicken. Cover and cook on high for 3 to 4 hours or on low for 6 to 8 hours. Serve over rice, mashed potatoes, or noodles with fresh parsley or tarragon on top.

෴ ෴ ෴

Here's another fancy one, and it came from my BFF again (no, not Susan, the slow cooker!) Can you believe it? I don't think the French would approve, but who cares! It's really good!

෴ ෴ ෴

Crockpot Brats

12 to 16 fresh brats

1 jar (32 ounces) sauerkraut

2 medium apples, peeled and finely chopped

1/4 cup packed brown sugar

1/4 cup finely chopped onion

1 cup apple juice

1 bottle (12 ounces) beer

4 tablespoons butter

12 to 16 brat buns or hard rolls, split

Lightly grill or fry the brats to brown for a minute or two. Dump the next 7 ingredients on top. Cover and cook on low for 4 to 5 hours or high for 2 to 3 hours. Place brats in buns, using a slotted spoon. You can top with sauerkraut and onions if you want.

∾ ∾ ∾

I think I mentioned a time or two that we really love our sausage and brats in Wisconsin. To be honest, I never had a brat 'til I moved here in college. I remember at first calling them "Bratz" like the dolls, or naughty little kids. Now I not only know how to pronounce them, I can't imagine life without them. Especially on game day! Try this recipe and you won't miss a play!

∾ ∾ ∾

Slow Cooker Italian Sausages

8 to 12 Italian sausages (sweet or hot)

2 jars (24 to 28 ounces) marinara sauce

1 cup dry red wine

2 large green bell peppers, sliced into thick strips

1 large onion, diced

1 teaspoon garlic salt

1 teaspoon dried basil

2 teaspoons sugar

1/2 teaspoon dried oregano

Grated parmesan cheese

8 to 12 brat buns, toasted

Brown sausages on the grill or in a skillet for a few minutes. Place sausages and vegetables in a slow cooker with remaining ingredients. Cook on low for 4 hours or on high for 2 to 3 hours. Serve sausages with a little sauce, peppers and onions on buns. Sprinkle with grated parmesan cheese. You can also serve them over hot cooked pasta with Parmesan cheese on top.

৩ ৩ ৩

This is another great game day or party recipe! If you're tired of brats, (and, yes it does happen every once in awhile) make this! Italian sausages are so good!!! Something just a little different. CAUTION! If you are serving these in buns they are messy!! Make sure you've got lots of napkins!

৩ ৩ ৩

Easiest Ever Slow Cooker Chicken Soup

3 to 4 carrots, peeled and cut into chunks

1 large onion, chopped

4 stalks celery, cut into chunks

4 to 6 boneless, skinless chicken breast halves

Salt and pepper

8 to 10 cups chicken stock

1 tablespoon dried parsley

Egg noodles or rice

2 tablespoons of chopped Italian parsley

Put carrots, onions, and celery into crock pot. Season chicken with salt and pepper and place it over the vegetables. Pour in stock and sprinkle parsley on top. Cover and cook on low for 6 to 8 hours or high for 3 to 4 hours. Use a fork to shred chicken into big pieces. Serve chicken, broth and veggies in bowls with hot cooked rice or noodles. Sprinkle chopped parsley on top.

∾ ∾ ∾

Do you know it's just going to be "one of those days?" Maybe the kids have a cold, and you've got tons going on. Hurry up and get this in the slow cooker in the morning. See, the day wasn't that bad! Chicken soup makes it all better!

∾ ∾ ∾

Cheese and Sausage Chowder

1 pound smoked sausage, cut into 1/2" slices

4 cups frozen O'Brien potatoes or southern style cubed hash brown potatoes

1 tablespoon dried minced onion

1 can (15 ounces) green beans, drained

1 box (16 ounces) processed cheese, cut in cubes

3 to 4 cups milk

2 cans (10.75 ounces) cream of celery soup

Dash hot sauce

Splash of beer (optional)

Shredded cheddar cheese

Chopped scallions

Place the sausage, potatoes, minced onion, green beans, soup, hot sauce and 3 cups of milk into a slow cooker. Put the cheese on top. Cover and cook on low for 2 to 3 hours, stirring often. If too thick, add another cup or more of milk. You can throw a splash of beer in there to at the end to thin it out just a bit. Serve with extra cheddar cheese and chopped scallions on top.

∿ ∿ ∿

We LOVE our cheese and our sausage in Wisconsin. And, our beer too!!! I knew this would be a winner! I made it on my show and everybody went crazy over it. One of my facebook friends told me to add a splash of beer at the end. GREAT IDEA!! I should have thought of that! Well, I guess you can't think of everything. This is great on game day! Serve it with bread for dunking! Just yummy!

∿ ∿ ∿

"WHAT'S FOR DINNER? I'M HUNGRY!"

The first thing my kids say when they walk in the door after school.

Bacon Wrapped Stuffed Chicken Breasts

4 whole boneless, skinless chicken breasts, pounded thin

Salt and pepper

4 pieces of thick cut bacon

2 cups fresh baby spinach

1 cup crumbled feta cheese

2 tablespoons olive oil

Plain wooden toothpicks

Season chicken breasts on both sides with a little salt and pepper. Lay a half cup of spinach on chicken breasts. Crumble a few tablespoons of feta on top of the spinach. Roll up tightly. Wrap bacon strip around each chicken breast. Secure with toothpick. In a large oven proof skillet heat oil. Brown chicken breasts for a few minutes on each side. Place skillet in a 375 degree preheated oven and bake for 20 to 30 minutes, until chicken is done and juices run clear.

❧ ❧ ❧

She had me at bacon! WOW! These are good!! Gotta thank Packers' wife Andrea Collins for this one. She came over to my house to make these and I've been making them ever since.

❧ ❧ ❧

222

Almond Apricot Chicken

6 skinless, boneless chicken breast halves or 1 whole cut up fryer

1 envelope dry onion soup mix

1 bottle (8 ounces) Russian salad dressing

1 cup apricot preserves

1/2 cup water

1/4 cup sliced almonds (optional, as always, if you don't do nuts)

Preheat oven to 350 degrees. Place chicken pieces in a 9" × 13" dish that has been sprayed with cooking spray. Whisk the onion soup mix, dressing, preserves and water together, and pour over the chicken. Cover dish with foil and bake for 60 minutes. Uncover and sprinkle the almonds on top of chicken and bake another 15 to 30 minutes until the chicken gets a little browned and the nuts get toasted.

〜 〜 〜

Okay, it really doesn't get much easier than this! You can throw this together in two minutes. Get it in the oven and go take a nice hot bath! You deserve it! Just don't drop the book you're reading in the tub! I hate it when that happens! (So does the library and your wallet!!!) We like this with wild rice or rice pilaf (the boxed stuff) and some veggies like broccoli or zucchini.

〜 〜 〜

Orange Chipotle Roasted Chicken

1 whole chicken, cleaned and patted dry

Half a can (7 ounces) chipotle peppers in Adobo sauce

2 tablespoons honey

2 tablespoons brown sugar

2 oranges, sliced

Salt and pepper

Preheat oven to 375 degrees. Place the chicken in a deep roasting pan. Season it well with salt and pepper. Combine the chipotle peppers, honey and brown sugar in a bowl and rub the chicken with this mixture. Place the orange segments inside of the chicken. Roast for 45 to 60 minutes or until internal temperature reaches 165 degrees.

∞ ∞ ∞

Bored with the same 'ole chicken recipes! Me too sometimes! Here's a fun, new one for you! It's got a little kick to it, but not too much. Don't want to do a whole chicken, no worries. Just throw the sauce over chicken pieces or chicken breasts and squeeze a little fresh orange juice over it. It's great with my Cheesy Green Chili Potatoes in the "What's on the Side?" chapter and a simple salad of sliced avocados and tomatoes drizzled with olive oil and a squeeze of lime juice.

∞ ∞ ∞

Greek Baked Chicken

4 to 6 split bone-in chicken breasts or one whole cut up fryer

1/2 cup olive oil

Juice from 2 lemons

1 tablespoon dried oregano

4 cloves garlic, chopped

Salt and pepper

1/2 cup pitted kalamata olives

2 to 3 tomatoes, seeded and chopped

1 cup crumbled feta cheese

Whisk together oil, lemon juice, garlic, oregano and a little salt and pepper. Pour over the chicken. Cover and let marinate in the fridge for 8 hours or better yet overnight. Preheat oven to 400 degrees. Remove chicken from the marinade and place in a roasting pan. Season chicken with a little salt and pepper. Bake uncovered for 35 minutes. Take out of oven and sprinkle olives and tomatoes over chicken. Bake another 15 to 25 minutes until chicken is cooked through and juices run clear. Sprinkle feta cheese on top the minute the chicken comes out of the oven.

෫ ෫ ෫

I absolutely love Greek food! I was lucky enough to go to Greece in high school and one of these days I am going back. Until then, I make this chicken, serve it with rice or couscous, and a salad with my Greek Vinaigrette dressing (it's in the "Super Salads" chapter) and I kind of feel like I'm on the island of Santorini. Well sort of!

෫ ෫ ෫

Honey Baked Chicken

1/4 cup soy sauce

1/4 cup orange juice or water

1 cup honey

Pinch red pepper flakes (optional)

1 whole chicken, cut up

Whisk first 4 ingredients together. Line a 9" x 13" pan with foil. Spray foil with cooking spray. Place chicken in the pan. Pour honey mixture over the chicken, turn the chicken to coat with the sauce. Bake in a preheated 425 degree oven for 40 to 55 minutes or until chicken is cooked through and juices run clear.

࿊ ࿊ ࿊

Got chicken, soy sauce, and honey? Talk about a quick fix! Really tasty too. Kids love it! You can use 6 to 8 boneless chicken breasts too instead of a whole chicken. So, come on get this in the oven, there's a load of laundry to do! Is the laundry ever really done?? Not in my house!

࿊ ࿊ ࿊

Baked Chicken Parmesan

4 boneless, skinless chicken breasts halves, pounded thin

2 teaspoons garlic salt

1/2 teaspoon black pepper

1/2 cup flour

2 eggs

1 tablespoon of water

1 cup seasoned Italian bread crumbs

3 tablespoons olive oil

2 to 3 cups marinara sauce

2 cups shredded mozzarella

1/2 cup grated parmesan, divided

Season chicken with garlic salt and pepper. In a shallow dish (I use a pie plate) whisk eggs and water together. Put the flour in another shallow dish. Then in a third dish mix together the bread crumbs and 1/4 cup Parmesan cheese. First dredge the chicken pieces in the flour. Then dip them in the egg mixture. Next roll them in the breadcrumbs and parmesan so that they are well coated.   Heat oil in a large skillet. Add the breaded chicken and cook just until brown, about 2 minutes per side. Transfer chicken into a casserole dish that has been sprayed with cooking spray. Spoon a little marinara sauce over chicken. Top with shredded mozzarella and then sprinkle on the remaining 1/4 cup parmesan cheese. Bake in a preheated 375 degree oven until the cheese is bubbly and slightly browned and the chicken is cooked through, about 20 to 35 minutes. Serve with hot cooked pasta as a side.

Italian Chicken Bundles

2 boneless, skinless chicken breast halves, pounded slightly thin

1/2 teaspoon garlic salt

2 teaspoons dried Italian seasoning, divided

1/4 teaspoon black pepper

2 tablespoons pesto sauce

1 cup fresh baby spinach

2 tablespoons chopped sundried tomatoes

2 pieces of fontina or provolone cheese

1/2 a package (17.5 ounces) frozen puff pastry sheets, (one sheet), thawed

1 egg

3 tablespoons water

Preheat oven to 375. Place sprayed foil or parchment paper on a baking sheet. Season chicken on both sides with garlic salt, pepper and 1 teaspoon Italian seasoning. Cut the puff pastry sheet in half. Place 1/2 cup spinach in the center of each puff pastry sheet. Next place chicken on top of spinach. Spread 1 tablespoon pesto over chicken breast. Then layer with sundried tomatoes and top with cheese. Fold pastry sheet around chicken, using fingers or fork to seal the seams. Place seam side down on baking sheet. Whisk egg and water together. Brush a little on each puff pastry bundle. Sprinkle with an extra teaspoon of Italian seasoning. Bake 35 to 50 minutes. Serves 2.

Cherry Chicken Marsala

1/2 cup dried cherries

1/2 cup marsala wine

3 tablespoons olive oil, divided

4 boneless, skinless chicken breast halves, pounded slightly thin

2 teaspoons garlic salt

1 teaspoon black pepper

1/2 cup flour

2 tablespoons butter

2 tablespoons finely chopped onion

1 cup chicken stock

1/4 cup heavy cream

1 tablespoon cold butter

2 tablespoons fresh chopped Italian parsley

Combine cherries and marsala in a small saucepan and carefully heat for a few minutes. You can also place both in a small glass bowl and heat in microwave for 30 seconds. Season chicken with garlic salt and pepper. Dredge chicken in flour. Heat 2 tablespoons of oil in a large skillet over medium-high heat. Add chicken, cook 5 to 8 minutes on each side or until done and juices run clear. Remove chicken from pan to a plate and cover plate with foil to keep the chicken warm. Add the other tablespoon of oil to pan. Add onions and cook on low for a couple minutes until tender. Stir in stock, scraping the bottom of the pan to loosen up the browned bits. Add cherry marsala mixture and bring to a boil. Reduce heat to medium and simmer a few minutes. Add cream and continue to cook a few minutes until sauce is slightly thick. Season sauce with a little salt and pepper if needed. Turn off heat and whisk in butter. Serve chicken with sauce on the top. Garnish with fresh parsley. Great with rice pilaf or wild rice.

Lemon Artichoke Chicken

4 boneless, skinless chicken breast haves, pounded slightly thin

1/2 cup flour

1 teaspoon black pepper

2 teaspoons garlic salt

4 tablespoons butter, divided

1 tablespoon olive oil

1½ cups chicken stock

1/2 cup dry white wine or more stock

1 can (15 ounces) artichoke hearts quartered, drained

2 tablespoons capers

Juice from half a lemon

2 tablespoons chopped Italian parsley

In shallow dish, combine flour, garlic salt and black pepper. Dredge chicken breast halves in the flour mixture. In large skillet heat 2 tablespoons of butter and the olive oil. Sauté chicken over medium heat turning once, until lightly golden brown on both sides and cooked through, about 5 to 8 minutes per side. Remove chicken from pan and keep warm on a plate covered with foil. Add chicken stock and wine to pan, stirring to scrape bits off bottom. Bring mixture to a boil and simmer for a few minutes until it reduces a bit. Stir in lemon juice, artichoke hearts, and capers. Cook for a minute. Turn off heat and whisk in remaining 1 tablespoon cold butter and chopped parsley. Pour hot sauce and artichokes over chicken breasts. Great with buttered pasta. We love it with angel hair or fettuccini.

Skillet Cordon Bleu

4 boneless, skinless chicken breast halves

Salt and pepper

3 tablespoons butter

1/2 cup dry white wine or chicken stock

1 can (10.75 ounces) condensed cream of chicken soup

1 cup milk

8 thin slices of deli ham

1 cup shredded Swiss cheese

1 tablespoon chopped Italian parsley

Season chicken with a little salt and pepper. Heat the butter in a large skillet. Cook chicken in skillet until brown on both sides and juices run clear. Remove chicken from skillet and set aside. Add wine or stock to the pan. Turn up heat and bring to a simmer, stirring up any of those great brown bits on the bottom. Add soup and milk and whisk until smooth. If sauce gets a little too thick add a little more milk. Add chicken back to the pan. Top each piece with 2 slices of ham. Sprinkle 1/4 cup of cheese on top of ham. Cover skillet and cook for a few minutes until cheese melts. Garnish with parsley. Great with hot cooked buttered egg noodles or rice.

つ つ つ

I LOVE cordon bleu anything!! The French got this one right! Chicken, ham and Swiss cheese! It's all good. This one is a super quick fix. Need to get dinner on the table in 15 minutes or less? Get busy! Make this!

つ つ つ

Champagne Chicken

1/2 cup flour

2 teaspoons garlic salt

Salt and pepper

4 boneless, skinless chicken breast halves, pounded thin

4 tablespoons butter, divided

1 tablespoon olive oil

2 teaspoons dried tarragon

1/2 cup dry or brut champagne or sparkling wine (make sure it's not the sweet stuff!)

1/2 cup chicken stock

8 ounces fresh sliced mushrooms

1/2 cup heavy cream

Combine flour, garlic salt, and a little pepper in a shallow dish. Dredge (love that word! It's just a fancy word for dip or dunk) chicken in flour mixture. Heat 2 tablespoons butter and the olive oil on medium heat in a large skillet. Add chicken and cook about 5 to 8 minutes on each side until cooked through and juices run clear. Remove chicken to a plate. Cover chicken with foil to keep warm. Add remaining butter and mushrooms to the skillet. Sauté for a few minutes. Season with salt and pepper. Carefully (especially if you have a gas cook top) add champagne, chicken stock, and tarragon to the skillet. Bring to a boil. Turn down the heat a bit and let simmer for a few minutes until the sauces reduce down and starts to thicken a bit. Add cream and simmer another few minutes. Season the sauce with salt and pepper if needed. Spoon mushrooms and sauce over the chicken breasts. Great with wild rice or mashed potatoes as a side dish.

Southern Fried Chicken Breasts

3 eggs

2 cups flour

2 teaspoons pepper

2 teaspoons seasoning salt

2 teaspoons garlic powder

2 teaspoon salt

1/4 teaspoon cayenne

6 boneless skinless chicken breast halves

2 cups vegetable oil

Beat eggs in one mixing bowl. Mix flour and seasoning in a separate bowl. Dip the chicken in the egg then into the flour, covering evenly. Warm vegetable oil in a big skillet. Place floured chicken breast into oil (should sizzle or it's not hot enough). Brown for about 8 minutes each side of the chicken, until the chicken is golden brown and cooked through. Place on paper towels to soak up the grease.

∽ ∽ ∽

Southern gal, and all round really nice lady, Packers' wife, Candy Clifton came to my house and we made this. It's her secret family recipe. They use boneless chicken, but you can use a cut up fryer too. Good stuff! Thanks Candy!

∽ ∽ ∽

Crispy Baked Parmesan Chicken Strips

1 box (6 ounces) seasoned croutons, crushed

3/4 cup grated parmesan cheese

1 tablespoon dried parsley

1/2 teaspoon garlic salt

2 eggs

1/4 cup water

4 to 6 boneless, skinless chicken breast halves, cut in strips

Mix first 4 ingredients together in a shallow dish or pie plate. In a separate dish whisk the eggs and water together. Dip the chicken pieces into the egg wash and then roll in the crumbs. Place on jelly roll pan or cookie sheet that has been sprayed with cooking spray. Bake in preheated 400 degree oven for 12 to 20 minutes, until the chicken is cooked through, and the strips are golden and crispy. Serve with ranch dressing or your favorite dipping sauce.

෴ ෴ ෴

What kid doesn't like chicken strips? I sure don't think I've ever met one! Actually Bob and I love them too so when I make these everybody's happy! These are so much better that the frozen ones!! We're talking real chicken, not the pressed stuff! Have the kids help make these. Yeah, I know, we're talking croutons and parmesan all over the floor but hey that's what vacuums and dogs are for, right?

෴ ෴ ෴

My Mom's Favorite Chicken and Veggie Kabobs

1 ¾ cups bottled Italian salad dressing (we like Wish-bone)

2/3 cups Western dressing

4 to 6 boneless, skinless chicken breast halves, cut in 1 inch pieces.

4 to 6 cups vegetables (bell pepper pieces, red onion pieces, zucchini pieces, cherry tomatoes, and mushrooms)

skewers

Stir together both dressings. Alternately thread pieces of chicken and veggies on the skewers. Place the kabobs in a 9" x 13" glass pan. Pour all but about a half cup of the marinade over the kabobs. Turn kabobs to coat. Refrigerate the extra reserved marinade in a covered container. Cover the kabobs with plastic wrap and refrigerate for or up to 24 hours. Remove kabobs from marinade. Grill or broil kabobs, turning and basting with the extra reserved marinade, until vegetables are tender and chicken is cooked through.

ᘯ ᘯ ᘯ

When the whole gang gets together in Michigan in the summer, this is our FAVORITE dinner! No question about it! My mom used to pay big bucks for these kabobs at a fancy meat market near out cottage. Then one day I got smart and asked the butcher what all was in the "secret" marinade. Well, the secret's out now! I can't believe all that time and it was just TWO ingredients! Why didn't I ask earlier! Don't ever be afraid to ask! All they can say is no, right? Serve these over wild rice with a big salad and dessert and everybody goes to bed full and happy ready for waterskiing on Walloon the next day!

ᘯ ᘯ ᘯ

Dog Gone Good Meatloaf

2½ pounds ground beef

1/2 cup onion, finely diced

1 cup fresh breadcrumbs (just white bread that you put in the food processor or crumble by hand)

2 tablespoons Dijon mustard

1/4 cup milk

2 eggs, beaten

1 tablespoon garlic salt

2 teaspoons black pepper

3 tablespoons fresh chopped Italian parsley or 1 tablespoon dried parsley

1¾ cups ketchup, divided

3 tablespoons brown sugar

Dash Worcestershire sauce

8 strips bacon

Preheat oven to 425 degrees. Mix first 9 ingredients and ¼ cup of ketchup in a large bowl and use your hands to combine (don't over mix). If mixture seems a little dry, add more milk. Too loose, add more breadcrumbs. Put mixture into a 9" × 13" baking pan and form into a loaf shape. In a bowl, mix 1½ cups ketchup, brown sugar, and Worcestershire. Spoon over the meatloaf. Cover top of loaf with bacon, laying strips side by side. Bake on the middle rack for the first 20 minutes to sear the bacon and help it get crispy. Lower the oven heat to 375 degrees and bake another 30 to 50 minutes, or until thermometer reads 160 degrees. Pour off the grease and let it sit at least 10 minutes before cutting.

∾ ∾ ∾

This meatloaf got it's name because our dog, Levi, thought it was so Dog Gone Good!!! GOOD and GONE that is! Yep, I made it and left it on the counter for just a minute (I swear!) I went to do something quick, and the meatloaf was gone when I got back. That naughty dog! He had never done that before! But, okay what was I thinking, leaving that yummy meatloaf right there for him to drool over. Well, it wasn't funny then, but we can laugh about it now. WARNING!! Keep this meatloaf away from the dog but definitely make it cause it's really good!

∾ ∾ ∾

Nana's Meatloaf

2 pounds ground beef

1 envelope dry onion soup mix

2 large eggs, beaten

1 cup bread crumbs (or more if too moist. Nana never measured. She usually used crumbled up sandwich bread)

2 tablespoons water

1½ cups ketchup, divided

2 teaspoons dried parsley

1 can (3 ounces) French fried onions

Preheat oven to 350 degrees. In a large bowl, combine beef, dry soup mix, eggs, 1/2 cup ketchup, water and bread crumbs. Place mixture in a 9" × 13" pan that's been sprayed with cooking spray and form into a large loaf. Spread remaining ketchup over meatloaf. Sprinkle with parsley. Bake for 45 to 55 minutes. Top with French fried onions. Bake another 10 to 20 minutes.

ᗠ ᗠ ᗠ

Nana was Mimi's mother, my mom's grandmother, and my great-grandmother. She lived with us growing up. My mom worked so Nana was the one who cooked dinner most nights, that is until I found my way into the kitchen. Man, was she a good cook! Nothing fancy, just great home cookin' like pot roast and pork chops. She was known for her meatloaf and her lemon meringue pie. Never did get that pie recipe. Darn!

ᗠ ᗠ ᗠ

Swedish Meatloaf with Mushroom Sauce

2 pounds ground beef

1 cup fresh breadcrumbs

1 envelope dry onion soup mix

2 eggs, beaten

1/2 cup milk

Pinch nutmeg

8 ounces sliced mushrooms

4 tablespoons butter

Salt and pepper

1 tablespoons flour

2 cups chicken broth

1 sour cream

1 tablespoon fresh chopped dill or 2 teaspoons dried dill weed

Salt and pepper to taste

Preheat oven to 350 degrees. In bowl, combine first 6 ingredients and mix well. If too dry, add a little more milk or water. Put into a 9" x 13" baking dish that's been sprayed with cooking spray and form into a loaf. Bake for 50 to 60 minutes. While meatloaf is baking, sauté mushrooms and butter in a skillet until they just start to get tender. Season them with a little salt and pepper. Sprinkle flour over the mushrooms. Cook 1 minute stirring constantly. Gradually whisk in chicken broth and cook over medium heat, whisking until thick and bubbly. Turn down the heat and whisk in sour cream and dill. If sauce is too thick add a little more stock or some water or milk. Serve over warm sliced meatloaf. Perfect with my perfect mashed potatoes recipe! Also great with buttered noodles on the side!

Mimi's Famous Beef Stroganoff

2 pounds beef tenderloin or sirloin, cut 1 to 2 inch pieces

Salt and pepper

3/4 cup flour

2 tablespoons olive oil or a little more if needed

3 tablespoons butter

1 cup onions, finely diced

8 ounces sliced mushrooms

1 tablespoon tomato paste

2 tablespoons cognac (optional)

2 cups beef stock

2 cups cup sour cream

Hot cooked egg noodles

2 tablespoons chopped Italian parsley

Season beef well with salt and pepper and toss the pieces of beef in flour. In a large skillet heat oil and quickly brown beef for a minute or two on both sides. Don't overcrowd the pan. It works best to brown the beef in batches, adding more oil if needed. Remove beef to a plate. Add butter, onions and mushrooms to the same skillet you cooked the beef in and cook a few minutes until they start to get soft. Season them with a little salt and pepper. Add tomato paste and beef stock. Simmer for a few minutes until sauce starts to reduce a bit. Whisk in cognac and sour cream until smooth. Taste to see if sauce needs a little salt and pepper. If sauce gets too thick, add a little more beef stock or a splash of milk. Add beef back to the skillet just to heat. Serve immediately over warm noodles. Garnish with parsley.

No Peek Beef (The easy way to do stroganoff!)

2 pounds lean stew beef, cut into 2 inch pieces

1 envelope dry onion soup mix

1 can (10.75 ounces) of cream of mushroom soup

2 cups sour cream

1 cup milk

1/2 cup of dry red or white wine

8 ounces of sliced mushrooms

In a big bowl whisk together mushroom soup, onion soup mix, wine, milk, and sour cream. Mix in beef and mushrooms. Place in a casserole dish that's been sprayed with cooking spray and bake covered in a 300 degree oven for 2½ to 3 hours, until the meat is nice and tender. You can also cook this in a slow cooker. Cover and cook on low for 8 to 12 hours or on high for 5 to 6 hours. No peeking! (why, I don't know!) Great served over noodles, rice or mashed potatoes.

೧ ೧ ೧

If you like beef stroganoff (and I really do!) you will love this! Super easy, super good! Just takes awhile to do its thing in the oven or slow cooker, but it's worth the wait, trust me!

೧ ೧ ೧

My Favorite Steak Marinade

1/3 cup soy sauce

2 tablespoons sherry

1/4 cup honey

2 tablespoons canola oil

2 to 3 cloves garlic, chopped

Whisk all ingredients together. Pour over steaks turning to coat both sides. Marinate steaks for at least 4 hours or up to 24 hours. Remove from marinade, pat steaks dry and grill. Makes enough to marinate 2 to 4 smaller steaks or one big (1½ to 2 lb) flank steak.

ɷ ɷ ɷ

I LOVE, LOVE, LOVE this marinade! Especially with a nice flank steak. If you are using a flank, definitely marinate it for 24 hours. Grill your steak and let it rest for 5 minutes before you slice it diagonally against the grain into thin strips. Just yummy!

ɷ ɷ ɷ

Stuffed Bacon and Bleu Beef Tenderloin

1 8 to 10 inch center cut beef tenderloin

1 cup crumbled gorgonzola or bleu cheese

8 strips of bacon, cooked and crumbled

3 tablespoons olive oil

2 to 3 teaspoons garlic salt

2 teaspoons black pepper

2 tablespoons fresh chopped rosemary

Kitchen string or plain wooden toothpicks

1 cup aged balsamic vinegar (optional)

Heat oven to 425 degrees. Make a cut down the side of the beef to make a pocket but do not cut all the way through. Flip over and season the pocket with some garlic salt and pepper. Stuff with bacon and cheese. Close the pocket to keep the stuffing in with plain wooden toothpicks or kitchen string. Drizzle the roast with oil. Season well with garlic salt, pepper and rosemary. Bake in a roasting pan uncovered 30 to 40 minutes until thermometer reads 130 degrees (for medium rare) or higher if you like it more well done. Remove from the oven and cover with foil. Let rest for 10 to 15 minutes before slicing. (Remember meat will continue to cook even when it's out of the oven!) While beef is cooking, pour balsamic vinegar in a sauce pan. Simmer over medium heat to reduce down and thicken. Remove the toothpicks or cut the string. Slice the tenderloin into one inch pieces. Drizzle balsamic over beef before serving.

Italian Stuffed Flank Steak

1 large (1½ to 3 pound) beef flank steak

Salt and pepper

1 package (5 ounces) garlic herb cheese (Boursin)

2 cups fresh baby spinach

1/2 cup sun dried tomatoes packed in olive oil

Plain wooden toothpicks or kitchen string

2 tablespoons olive oil

1 tablespoon Italian seasoning

With a meat mallet, pound out steak a bit to make it as large as possible. Sprinkle steak with a little with salt and pepper. Spread cheese all over one side of the steak. Next, put spinach and sun dried tomatoes on top of the cheese. Roll up steak from short side. This will give you a long, stuffed flank steak. Secure with toothpicks or tie with kitchen string. Drizzle olive oil over the steak and season with Italian seasoning and a little more salt and pepper. Grill, turning occasionally or roast in jelly roll pan in a preheated 425 degree oven for 20 to 35 minutes or until an internal temperature of 125 to 130 degrees for medium rare. Let the steak rest for about 5 to 7 minutes before slicing into one inch pieces. This is really nice with some aged balsamic vinegar drizzled over the top.

New York Strip Steaks with a Gorgonzola Crust

3 tablespoons butter

1/4 cup gorgonzola cheese

1 clove garlic, minced

Freshly cracked black pepper

1/2 cup panko Japanese style bread crumbs

2 New York strip steaks

2 tablespoons olive oil

Kosher salt and black pepper

1 tablespoon fresh rosemary

To prepare the crust, put butter, garlic and gorgonzola in a small microwave safe bowl and microwave on high for 30 to 45 second until cheese and butter are melted. Stir in bread crumbs and set aside. Coat steaks lightly with oil and season both sides with salt, pepper and rosemary. Grill or fry steaks for a couple minutes on each side. Transfer to a roasting pan. Spread crumb mixture on top of both sides. Roast in preheated 450 degree oven for 5 to 10 minutes or more, using a meat thermometer so that steaks are done the way you like them.

ෆ ෆ ෆ

Okay, you'd pay big bucks for this at a restaurant! So, make these at home and, then there's more money left for shopping! Like, most gals, I LOVE to shop! This is a quick, easy, but kind on fancy date night fix! Also, great when company's coming. Serve this with my Caesar salad and my roasted garlic mashers and, man we're talking about a seriously good dinner

ෆ ෆ ෆ

New York Strip Steaks with Peppercorn Cream Sauce

2 tablespoons whole black peppercorns, crushed

2 teaspoons garlic salt

2 New York strip steaks

2 tablespoons butter

1 tablespoon Worcestershire sauce

2 tablespoons brandy

1 teaspoon fresh ground black pepper (or more if you like it peppery)

1 cup heavy cream

1 tablespoon fresh chopped Italian parsley

Combine peppercorns and garlic salt and rub over both sides of steak. Heat oil in a large skillet. Add steaks and sear on both sides until they are done the way you like them. Remove steaks to a plate and cover to keep warm. Add butter, brandy, cream and worcestershire to the skillet. Simmer for a few minutes to thicken sauce. Stir in chopped parsley. Serve sauce over steaks.

෨ ෨ ෨

Did I mention I'm a "sauce" person? I think I did. Hey why not be like the chefs in the restaurants and make a quick pan sauce. It's easy to do once you get the hang of it. It's the way to really take dish or in this case an ordinary steak to the next level! So, just like the Nike commercial says, "just do it!"

෨ ෨ ෨

Rib Eye Steaks with Green Chili Cream Sauce

2 teaspoons ground cumin

1 tablespoon garlic salt

1 tablespoon chili powder

2 teaspoons black pepper

4 rib eye steaks

2 tablespoons butter

1/4 onion, finely diced

1 to 2 cloves garlic, minced

1 can (4 ounces) diced green chilies

1/4 cup chicken stock

1 cup heavy cream

1 lime

1 cup shredded monterey jack cheese or pepper jack cheese

2 tablespoons chopped fresh cilantro

Mix first 4 ingredients together. Place steaks in a glass pan and rub spice mixture into both sides of the meat. Cover with plastic wrap and refrigerate for 2 to 8 hours. For the sauce heat the butter in a skillet. Cook onion in the butter until the onion gets soft. Add garlic. Cook for 30 seconds, stirring constantly. Turn up heat and add the can of green chiles, cream and stock. Let sauce simmer and reduce down until it thickens a bit. Before grilling the steaks drizzle them with a little olive oil. Grill steaks to your liking. Take off the grill and squeeze a little fresh lime juice over the steaks. Spoon a little sauce on top. Next, sprinkle with a little cheese and cilantro.

Greek Ribeyes

2 ribeye steaks

1/4 cup olive oil

2 tablespoons red wine vinegar

2 teaspoons dried oregano

2 cloves fresh minced garlic

Salt and pepper

1/4 cup feta cheese, crumbled

1 tablespoon pitted kalamata olives, chopped

Fresh lemon juice

Whisk together oil, vinegar, garlic and oregano. Pour marinade over the steaks and let marinate, covered in the fridge, for up to 24 hours. Remove steaks from marinade and pat dry. Season them with some salt and pepper. Grill or fry steaks until they are done the way you like them (I'm a medium-rare kind of gal). Sprinkle some feta cheese, a little lemon juice and some olives on top of the warm steaks. These are great served with couscous!

Grilled Burgundy Steaks with Butter

1 cup burgundy wine, divided

2 tablespoons canola oil

1 tablespoon Worcestershire sauce

1 tablespoon garlic, chopped

1 teaspoon fresh or 1/2 teaspoon dried thyme

4 beef tenderloin steaks

1 to 2 tablespoons olive oil

4 tablespoons butter, softened

1 tablespoon minced shallots

1 tablespoon fresh chopped parsley

Salt and pepper

1 to 2 tablespoons olive oil

Whisk together, all but 1 teaspoon of the wine, canola oil, Worcestershire, garlic and thyme. Pour the wine marinade over the steaks. Cover and let marinade in the fridge for a few hours or overnight. In a bowl, by hand, or with a food processor mix together butter, 1 teaspoon of the burgundy wine, shallots and parsley. Cover and refrigerate until ready to use. When ready to cook steaks, remove flavored butter and steaks from refrigerator. Pat steaks dry and season with a little salt and pepper. Drizzle steaks with a little olive oil and grill or pan fry steaks until they are done how you like them. Top hot steaks with a tablespoon of the butter mixture and serve right away.

Beef and Pineapple Kabobs

1/2 cup soy sauce

1/4 cup honey

2 tablespoons rice wine vinegar

1 teaspoon garlic powder

1 tablespoon fresh minced ginger

1/2 cup canola oil

2½ pounds beef tenderloin or sirloin steak, cut in 2 inch pieces

2 cups fresh pineapple chunks

2 green bell peppers, cut in 2-inch chunks

1 red onion, cut in 1 inch wedges

Skewers

Wisk first 6 ingredients together. Add beef and marinate covered in the fridge for several hours or better yet overnight. Remove the beef from the marinade and skewer it with the pineapple and veggies. Grill for 10 to 20 minutes, turning every once in awhile. If you are using wooden skewers make sure to soak them in water for a few hours so they don't burn.

ल ल ल

When I am craving a tropical vacation, but it's just not going to happen I put on my winter coat and head outside and grill these. These are also fun in the summer! Hey, why not have a luau!! We did that once. It was a blast! These would be perfect to serve!

ल ल ल

Carne Asada (Makes the Best Steak Fajitas!)

Juice of 1 lime

Juice of 1 lemon

Juice of 1 orange

2 tablespoons chili powder

1 tablespoon dried oregano

2 tablespoons ground cumin

1½ teaspoons crushed coriander seeds

5 garlic cloves

1/4 cup soy sauce

2 tablespoons vegetable oil

2 jalapeno pepper, sliced

1 medium onion, sliced thin

1 cup chopped fresh cilantro

1 large (1½ to 3 pound) beef flank steak

Warm flour tortillas and your favorite taco or fajita fixin's

Whisk together first 10 ingredients in a bowl. Stir in peppers, onion and cilantro. Pour the mixture over the steak. Cover and let it marinate in the fridge for 24 hours. I like to marinate in big plastic re-sealable bags. Sometimes I double bag it or put the bag in a glass dish just in case! Don't want that marinade all over my fridge! Remove steak from the marinade and grill, flipping once until it's done the way you like it.   I like it best medium rare, but that's me. Let steak rest about 5 minutes before slicing into thin strips diagonally against the grain. Serve steak in tortillas with your favorite taco or fajita fixin's.

Really Good Roasted Corned Beef and Cabbage

3 to 5 pound corned beef brisket (flat cut if they have it)

1 head of cabbage, cut in wedges

2 cups bag baby carrots

4 cups chicken stock

4 tablespoons whole grain mustard

3 tablespoons of honey

1 stick butter

1/4 teaspoon garlic salt

2 tablespoons fresh chopped dill

3 pounds baby red potatoes, boiled

Preheat oven to 350 degrees. Rinse off roast with cold water. Pat dry. Place in a roasting pan. If it comes with a seasoning packet, sprinkle that on top. Pour chicken stock over the roast and into the pan. Cover with foil and bake for about 3 to 5 hours until beef starts to get fork tender. Add cabbage and carrots to the roasting pan, cover with foil and bake another 30 to 45 minutes or so until carrots are just tender. Remove veggies from the pan to a bowl or serving platter. Cover with foil to keep warm. In a small bowl, mix mustard and honey together and spread on top of roast. Place beef under broiler for a few minutes to get it a little brown on top. Melt butter, dill and garlic salt together. Slice beef and serve with hot potatoes, cabbage and carrots with the dill butter drizzled on top.

Mediterranean Stuffed Peppers

1 pound ground beef

1 cup onion, finely, diced

2 teaspoons garlic salt

1 teaspoon black pepper

2 cloves garlic, minced

1 to 2 tablespoons olive oil

6 red, orange, or yellow bell peppers (or a couple of each), cored and tops removed

1½ to 2 cups cooked white rice

1 can (14.5 ounces) crushed tomatoes

2 tablespoons fresh chopped mint

8 ounces feta cheese, crumbled

Fresh chopped Italian parsley

Brown ground beef and onion with olive oil until no longer pink. Season with garlic salt and pepper. Stir in garlic and cook another 30 seconds. Stir in crushed tomatoes and rice. Remove from heat and add mint and half of the feta cheese. Drizzle the peppers with a little oil and season with some salt and pepper. Place peppers in baking pan that has been sprayed with cooking spray. Fill each pepper with the meat and rice mixture. Sprinkle the rest of the feta cheese and parsley on top of the peppers. Cover pan with aluminum foil. Bake at 350 degrees for 20 to 30 minutes, until peppers start to get soft. Remove foil and bake an extra 10 to 15 minutes until the top gets a little brown.

Just Peachy Pork Tenderloin

2 pork tenderloins

1 cup teriyaki sauce

1 cup peach preserves

8 slices of bacon

Plain wooden toothpicks

2 to 3 tablespoons butter

2 tablespoons chopped Italian parsley

Whisk together teriyaki sauce and peach preserves. Take half of the sauce and put it in a container. Cover and refrigerate. Pour the other half of the sauce over the tenderloins. Marinate pork covered in the fridge for a few hours, or even better, overnight. Before cooking remove tenderloins from marinade and wrap each with 4 slices of bacon. Secure with toothpicks. Put in roasting pan and roast in a preheated 400 degree oven for 35 to 45 minutes until the pork reaches an internal temperature of 160 degrees. Let rest covered with foil for 5 to ten minutes before slicing. While pork is resting, take that extra sauce you have in the fridge and heat that in a pan with the butter until warm. Spoon sauce over sliced pork. You can sprinkle some parsley on top if you want, but you don't have to.

෴ ෴ ෴

This is another one the kids really like! They love pork tenderloin and of course they like bacon, doesn't everybody? I invited some friends over for dinner and made this and yes, they asked for the recipe. LOVE THAT! Anyway, this is super simple to make and a real crowd pleaser. We like it with rice or couscous and a big salad.

෴ ෴ ෴

Grilled Rosemary Balsamic Pork Tenderloin

1/2 cup balsamic vinegar

1/2 cup olive oil

2 to 3 tablespoons of fresh chopped rosemary

3 cloves chopped fresh garlic

1/2 teaspoon fresh ground black pepper

1/2 teaspoon kosher salt

2 whole pork tenderloins

1/2 cup crumbled gorgonzola cheese (optional)

Whisk together first six ingredients. Place pork into a re-sealable plastic bag. Pour marinade over pork. Seal bag and marinade in refrigerator for 4 to up to 24 hours. Fire up the grill. Remove pork from bag and grill to internal temperature of 160 degrees. Place pork on a platter and sprinkle with gorgonzola cheese on top. Let rest a few minutes before slicing. Don't feel like grillin' you can roast the pork in a preheated 425 degree oven for 25 to 45 minutes.

∿ ∿ ∿

This is a really easy way to dress up pork tenderloin. I always have some balsamic vinegar and olive oil on hand. Don't have fresh rosemary, use a tablespoon of dried. Love the crumbled gorgonzola on top. I think you know by now that a little cheese on top makes a lot of things even better. A drizzle of aged balsamic vinegar on top may also be nice! This is great with a big salad and my roasted garlic mashers!

∿ ∿ ∿

Pork Tenderloin with Port Mustard Sauce

1 pound of pork tenderloin, sliced into 1/2 inch thick medallions

1/3 cup flour

Salt and pepper

1 to 3 tablespoons butter

1 to 3 tablespoons olive oil

1 cup chicken stock

2/3 cup port wine

2 tablespoons Dijon mustard

2 tablespoons chopped Italian parsley

Use a meat mallet (or if you don't have one the bottom of a frying pan) to flatten the medallions of pork a bit. Don't pound too thin! Sprinkle pork medallions with salt and pepper. Then coat with flour; shaking off excess. In a large skillet, heat 1 tablespoon of butter and oil. Cook pork over medium-high heat until cooked through and lightly browned, about 2 to 4 minutes per side. You will probably have to do this in batches with a little extra butter and oil. Don't over crowd the pan or your pork won't brown. Transfer pork to plate and cover with foil to keep warm. Add stock, port and mustards to skillet. Bring to a boil and let simmer for about 4 minutes until sauce thickens a bit. Serve over pork. Top with parsley.

∽ ∽ ∽

This is a really nice to make in the fall or during the holidays! Start out your dinner with my Apple Cranberry Salad in the "Super Salads" chapter and serve this with wild rice and you've got an extra special dinner! You don't have to buy really expensive port wine, a ten dollar bottle is just fine!

∽ ∽ ∽

Apple Dijon Pork Chops

4 pork chops

Salt and pepper

2 teaspoons fresh thyme or 1 teaspoon dried thyme

2 tablespoons olive oil

1 cup chicken stock

1 cup apple juice or cider

1/2 cup apple jelly

1 to 2 tablespoons Dijon mustard

1 tablespoon cold butter

Sprinkle both sides of the pork chops with thyme, salt and pepper. Heat oil in a large skillet over medium-high heat. Fry pork chops, flipping once until golden and just cooked through. Remove chops from the pan. Cover them with foil and set aside. Add the broth and juice. Bring to a boil. Simmer for a few minutes until the sauce starts to reduce down and thicken. Add jelly and mustard. Whisk until smooth. Turn off heat and whisk in butter. Return pork chops to pan and coat with the sauce. Spoon the extra sauce over pork chops. Great with mashed potatoes or wild rice!

Like they said on the Brady Brunch, "Pork Chops and Apple Sauce." Anybody else remember that episode? Oh, boy I'm getting old! Anyway, I did some research (why, cause I was curious) and way back when they started serving fruit with pork and meats to help it go down easier. That's how the whole pork chops served with apple sauce thing happened. I'm taking it to the next level here. It's still really easy and I think it might be better than Alice's.

Chili Lime Pork Roast

1/4 cup tablespoon olive oil

3 tablespoons lime juice

1 (3 to 4 pound) boneless pork loin roast

2 tablespoons chili powder

1 teaspoon ground cumin

1/2 teaspoon dried oregano

1 teaspoon black pepper

1 teaspoon garlic powder

1 teaspoon salt

Combine olive oil and lime juice. Put roast in a shallow glass pan. Pour olive oil and lime juice over roast. Combine remaining seasonings and rub the roast all over. Cover and refrigerate for at least 4 hours or overnight. Preheat oven to 350 degrees. Roast pork for 60 to 90 or until it reaches an internal temperature of 160 degrees. Let the roast rest for 10 minutes before slicing.

തമ തമ തമ

Okay, here's a fun one for you! When was the last time you made a pork roast? They are so easy. Enough chicken already! Make this! It's great with my cheesy green chili potatoes in the "What's on the Side" chapter!

തമ തമ തമ

Pork Souvlaki with Cucumber Sauce

6 garlic cloves, minced

1/2 cup olive oil

1/2 cup lemon juice

2 tablespoons oregano

2 teaspoon salt

1 teaspoon fresh ground pepper

2 to 3 pounds pork tenderloin, cut in 1 inch pieces

Whisk the first 5 ingredients together. Place pork in a glass bowl or in a re-sealable bag and pour the marinade over the top. Mix well. Seal the bag or cover the bowl and let marinate in the fridge 24 hours. Remove pork from the marinade. Skewer the pork. Grill until the pork is cooked through. Serve with cucumber sauce.

Cucumber Sauce:

1 tablespoons red wine vinegar

1 clove garlic, minced

1 cup Greek yogurt

1 cup sour cream

1½ cups cucumbers, seeded and finely diced

1 tablespoon chopped fresh mint

Mix all together and chill for at least two hours before serving.

Pineapple Mustard Ham Glaze

1 can (8 ounces) crushed pineapple

3 tablespoons of Dijon mustard

1/3 cup brown sugar

Mix it all together.   Brush on the ham several times the last hour of cooking.

෨ ෨ ෨

You just can't go wrong with a ham! Having a party? Ham is by far the easiest thing to serve! It's pretty much a done deal! You just need to warm it up in the oven. I always dress up my ham with a quick glaze. This one is so easy and delicious! You can decorate the ham like my Nana always used to with pineapple slices, cloves and maraschino cherries. We like to serve this with homemade mac n' cheese!

෨ ෨ ෨

~ ~ ~

They loved my glazed ham and homemade mac n' cheese at Golden House in Green Bay. My crew and I try to help out at the shelter and make dinner everyone once in awhile, especially during the holidays. They love it and we do too!

~ ~ ~

Brat Tub

One aluminum foil baking pan

3 to 4 bottles (12 ounces) of beer

1 stick of butter

2 medium onions, sliced

1 pound bag or jar or sauerkraut, drained

12 to 16 brats

Brat Buns or Hard rolls

Ketchup and mustard

Place pan on the grill over indirect heat. Add beer, kraut, butter and onions. Heat until the onions start to get nice and soft. Grill the brats and when they are done put them in the foil pan (Brat Tub) to keep warm. Serve brats with onions and kraut on top if you like them that way (and I do!)

∽ ∽ ∽

Everybody has their own way of doing brats in Wisconsin. I got hooked on doing it this way because that's how Mad Dog and Merrill do 'em. When it comes to grillin' these guys know what they're talking about! They also know how to have a good time!! See, you can have the brats all grilled up ahead of time and keep them all warm and cozy in the brat tub until everybody's ready to eat. LOVE THAT! Serve these with my jazzed up baked beans and apple slaw and you've got one great party!

∽ ∽ ∽

Philly Brats

1 box (16 ounces) processed cheese, cut in cubes

3 tablespoons milk

2 tablespoons mayonnaise

6 to 8 brats

3 tablespoons olive oil

1 small yellow onion, sliced thin

1 yellow pepper, sliced thin

1 green pepper, sliced thin

8 ounces sliced mushrooms

Salt and pepper

6 to 8 brat buns

In a saucepan or in the microwave, carefully melt cheese with milk and mayonnaise to make a cheese sauce. Stir until smooth and keep warm. (If cheese sauce gets too thick, add more milk). Heat the oil in a skillet. Cook veggies in the skillet until they just start to get soft. (If your grill has a side burner, USE IT!! Keeps the mess out of the kitchen!) Season the veggies with a little salt and pepper. While the veggies are cooking grill the brats. Place brats on bun and top with cheese sauce and vegetables.

∽ ∽ ∽

Like Philly cheesesteak sandwiches? Then, I think you'll like these too!   Brats and cheese, come on I'm a Cheesehead!! Love 'em both!! And together WOW! These are fun to serve during Packers games because they are Green and Gold. Go Pack!

∽ ∽ ∽

Brat Kabobs

1/2 cup soy sauce

6 ounces frozen apple juice concentrate, thawed

2 tablespoons apple cider vinegar

2 tablespoons Dijon mustard

1 red pepper, cut into 2" pieces

1 green pepper, cut into 2" pieces

1 yellow or orange pepper, cut into 2" pieces

1 red onion, cut into wedges

6 fresh brats

1 bottle (12 ounces) beer

1 cup water

Skewers (if they're wooden, make sure to soak em' in water for a few hours!)

Mustard for dipping (optional)

Whisk together soy sauce, apple juice concentrate, vinegar and mustard. Pour half of the sauce over the peppers and onions and let marinate for an hour. Set aside the rest of the sauce. Place brats in large pan. Add water and beer and simmer for about 10 minutes. Remove from pan and let cool slightly. Slice each brat into 5 equal pieces and thread onto metal or soaked wooden skewers with the marinated vegetables. Brush the kabobs with that reserved marinade and grill until veggies are tender and brats are golden brown, turning and basting frequently with reserved marinade. Serve with your favorite mustard on the side for dipping.

Shrimp on the Barbie

3 pounds medium to large raw shrimp, shell on

1 cup bottled Italian salad dressing (I like Wish-bone)

A few dashes hot sauce (or more if you like it spicy)

2 garlic cloves, minced

2 lemons

1/4 cup chopped fresh Italian parsley

1/2 cup butter, cut in pieces

Foil roasting pan

Crusty French Bread

Put shrimp, garlic, Italian dressing, hot sauce and butter in a foil pan. Squeeze juice from half a lemon over shrimp mixture. Toss to coat. Slice other half of that lemon into thin slices and add to pan. Place pan on grill on low to medium heat. Stir shrimp every few minutes. Grill for 10 to 25 minutes until shrimp turns pink. You can also bake shrimp in a preheated 350 degree oven. Stir in parsley when shrimp is done. Cut the other lemon into wedges. Serve shrimp with lemon wedges, extra hot sauce, and lots of napkins. Use the bread to sop up the sauce.

∾ ∾ ∾

People freak out over this shrimp! It's the easiest recipe and when it comes to cleaning up, gotta love those foil pans! This makes a perfect party starter! It also makes a great dinner!

∾ ∾ ∾

Shrimp and Sausage Boil

1/2 cup Old Bay Seasoning

2 tablespoons salt

4 quarts water

2 bottles (12 ounces) beer

16 to 24 baby red potatoes, washed well (if they are bigger, cut them in half)

16 small boiling onions

2 pounds smoked sausage, cut in 2 to 3 inch pieces

8 ears of corn on the cob, cut in half

4 pounds medium to large raw shrimp, in shells

2 to 3 pounds melted butter

2 to 3 lemons, cut in wedges

In a really big stock pot, bring Old Bay, salt, water and beer to a boil. Add potatoes and onions. Cook over high heat for 8 minutes. Add smoked sausage and corn and continue to cook for another 3 to 4 minutes. Add shrimp in shells and cook until shrimp turns pink, about 4 minutes. Drain cooking liquid. Serve everything or even pepper pour it all in the center of a picnic table covered with butcher paper. Serve it with warm melted butter, lemon wedges and lots and lots of napkins or a few rolls of paper towels. This makes enough for about 8 people.

∾ ∾ ∾

This is a summer time tradition at the cottage. Got a turkey deep fryer? It's perfect for a shrimp boil too! Why not keep all the mess outside! I always start out the night with some muchies like Mimi's crab dip or my seafood spread. Keeps everybody happy 'til dinner. Then I like to serve this with a big salad or coleslaw and crusty French bread.   It's just so fun. Take lots of pictures!! It's going to be a fun night! I bought a bunch of those little butter warmers like they have at the restaurants. Gotta have my butter warm.

∾ ∾ ∾

Shrimp and Artichoke Scampi

2 tablespoons olive oil

4 large cloves garlic, minced

1 pound medium to large shrimp, peeled and deveined

1 can (14 ounces) quartered artichoke hearts, drained

1 to 2 tablespoons capers (optional)

1/3 cup dry white wine (or chicken stock)

2 tablespoons fresh lemon juice

2 teaspoons lemon zest

2 tablespoons chopped Italian parsley

1/2 teaspoon salt

Pinch of red pepper flakes

Shredded or grated Parmesan cheese (optional)

Hot cooked pasta (We like it best with spaghetti or fettuccini)

Heat the oil in a large skillet over medium heat. Add garlic. Cook for 30 seconds. Add shrimp. Season shrimp with salt and red pepper flakes. Add artichoke hearts, capers, wine, and lemon juice and cook until the shrimp turn pink, about 3 to 4 minutes. Stir in the butter, lemon zest and 2 tablespoons of parsley. Spoon the shrimp, artichokes, and the extra sauce over hot cooked pasta. Serve with a little Parmesan cheese on top if you wan to. (I usually do!)

Lemon, artichokes, shrimp, pasta! What's not to like! If you want to serve shrimp but are watching your pennies, this is a great way to do it! You don't need a ton for this recipe. You can even use less than a pound if you want. Pasta is a great way to stretch that dollar! See mom, this is why I bought those capers!

Seafood Supreme

4 pieces white flaky fish (like cod or haddock)

1/2 pound uncooked, peeled and deveined shrimp

1/2 pound small to medium sized scallops (optional)

1 stick butter, cut into 8 pieces

2 tomatoes, seeded and diced

Salt and pepper

1 lemon

1 cup shredded sharp cheddar cheese

1 teaspoon paprika

4 large sheets, heavy duty foil

2 tablespoons chopped Italian parsley

Spray each foil sheet with cooking spray. Place a piece of fish on each sheet. Then place a few shrimp and scallops around the fish. Season seafood with a little salt and pepper. Cut lemon in half. Squeeze juice from one half of lemon on top of seafood. Divide the butter among the 4 packets. Sprinkle tomatoes and then cheese on top of seafood. Next sprinkle paprika on top. Wrap up packets (Not too tightly) and place on a hot grill for 12 to 20 minutes until shrimp are pink and scallops and fish are cooked through. Carefully open the hot packets. Garnish with fresh parsley and serve with other half of the lemon cut in wedges. You can also bake packets in the oven. Place packets on a jelly roll pan and bake in a preheated 400 degree oven for 15 to 20 minutes. Great with hot rice.

ल ल ल

I fell in love with dish at a local super club. And, just HAD to figure out a way to make it at home once in awhile too. By the way I'd never heard of a supper club before I came to Wisconsin. "What's a super club? Do you have to be a member to eat there?" That's what I remember asking myself. Anyway, I have come to LOVE, LOVE, LOVE Wisconsin supper clubs!!   And, no you don't have to be a member. They're just really good locally owned restaurants that usually serve up some of the best steaks and seafood around. And, at a great price! No need to dress up. Just come casual and hungry! Pull up a seat at the bar (if you can get one) and start up a conversation with the people next to you. You've never met them, but before long you've got some new friends. Another reason Bob and fell in love with Wisconsin!

ल ल ल

Italian Baked Fish

2 to 3 tablespoons olive oil

4 pieces of white flake (like cod, haddock, halibut, or sea bass)

1 can (14.5 ounces) diced tomatoes, drained or 1½ cups fresh diced tomatoes

2 tablespoons capers (optional)

2 cloves garlic, minced

2 tablespoons freshly squeezed lemon juice

1 teaspoon lemon zest

2 teaspoons dried Italian seasoning

1/4 cup dry white wine or chicken stock

Salt and pepper

Preheat oven to 400 degrees. Place fish in a baking dish sprayed with cooking spray. Drizzle fish fillets with oil. Season with a little salt, pepper and Italian seasoning. Add the tomatoes, capers, garlic, lemon juice, lemon zest and wine or stock. Bake for 15 to 25 minutes until the fish is white and flaky.

ᘐ ᘐ ᘐ

See, I don't always use butter in my recipes. Want to do something nice and light. Here you go! This is great over hot cooked rice pilaf and the "Layered Italian Salad" recipe in the "Super Salads" chapter.

ᘐ ᘐ ᘐ

Cheesy Baked Fish

4 pieces of white flaky fish (like cod or haddock)

2/3 cup mayonnaise

3 tablespoons butter, melted

1 tablespoon minced onion

1/4 cup grated Parmesan cheese

1 tablespoon fresh lemon juice

1/2 teaspoon Old Bay Seasoning

1/4 teaspoon black pepper

1/2 cup fresh bread crumbs

Fresh chopped dill or parsley

Lemon slices

Preheat oven to 400 degrees. Place fish in a 9" x 13" baking dish that's been sprayed with cooking spray. In a bowl, combine mayo, butter, onion, cheese, lemon juice, Old Bay and pepper. Mix until a thick paste is formed. Spread mixture evenly over fish filets, then top with bread crumbs. Bake for 15 to 25 minutes or until fish is completely cooked. To finish cooking, place fish under the broiler for another 2 to 3 minutes, or until top is golden brown. Garnish with fresh lemon slices and fresh dill or parsley.

∾ ∾ ∾

Okay, time to change things up! If you're a fish eater, this is a fun and easy way to dress it up! Just delicious! Great served with rice pilaf (just the boxed stuff) and veggies like asparagus on the side!

∾ ∾ ∾

Seafood in Puff Pastry

1 package of 6 frozen puff pastry shells

6 tablespoons butter, divided

1/2 pound medium shrimp, shelled and deveined

1/2 pound scallops

1/2 cup fresh lump crab meat or cooked lobster

1/4 cup red pepper, finely diced

1/4 cup celery, finely diced

1/2 teaspoon garlic powder

2 tablespoons all-purpose flour

1 cup milk

1/4 cup dry white wine or seafood stock

3/4 cup heavy cream

1/4 cup grated Parmesan cheese

1 tablespoon fresh lemon juice

2 tablespoons chopped fresh dill or Italian parsley

Bake pastry shells according to package directions. Melt 2 tablespoons of butter to a big skillet. Add shrimp and scallops and cook until they are just cooked through. Season them with a little salt and pepper. Remove seafood to a plate or bowl. Add remaining 4 tablespoons of butter to the skillet. Add celery and red pepper and cook for a few minutes until they start to get soft. Stir in flour and whisk constantly until combined with the veggies. Add wine or stock and milk. Cook, whisking often until sauce comes to a boil and thickens. Add cream and heat until warm but don't boil. Turn off heat, whisk in cheese. Stir in all the seafood, lemon juice and dill or parsley. If too thick add more milk or cream. Taste to see if more salt and pepper is needed. Split baked pastry shells in half. Spoon mixture on bottom half, and top with the other half shell.

Walnut Chicken Tortellini

2 tablespoons of olive oil

Salt and pepper

2 boneless, skinless chicken breast halves

1/4 cup walnuts (optional)

3 tablespoons Frangelico (hazelnut liqueur)

1 cup heavy cream

1 cup broccoli florets, steamed

1 package (9 ounces) refrigerated cheese tortellini, boiled

1/4 cup shredded Parmesan cheese

1 to 2 tablespoons chopped Italian parsley

Preheat the oven to 400 degrees. Heat oil in a big skillet. Season chicken with salt and pepper. Sear chicken on both sides for a few minutes. Remove chicken from the skillet and place in a pan and finish cooking it in the oven for another 7 to 15 minutes until it's cooked through. While chicken is cooking. Add Frangelico and cream to the skillet. Bring to a simmer and cook for a few minutes until it starts to thicken and reduce a bit. Stir in tortellini, broccoli and walnuts. Remove chicken from the oven and slice it into strips. Spoon pasta into big bowls or on to a plate. Put some sliced chicken on top. Sprinkle cheese and parsley on top.

෨ ෨ ෨

I was able to get this secret recipe from one of my chef friends. It was a best-seller on his menu. Hey, thanks Ryan!

෨ ෨ ෨

Bowtie Pasta with Chicken and Sundried Tomatoes

3 tablespoons olive oil, divided

2 to 3 teaspoons garlic salt

1/2 teaspoon black pepper

2 to 3 boneless, skinless chicken breast halves cut in 2 inch pieces

1/2 cup diced red and yellow pepper

2 garlic cloves, minced

2 teaspoons dried marjoram

1/2 cup dry white wine or chicken broth

1 cup chicken broth

3/4 cup heavy cream

1/4 cup diced sundried tomatoes

1 box (16 ounces) bow tie pasta, cooked al dente

1/2 cup shredded Parmesan cheese

2 to 3 tablespoons fresh chopped basil or Italian parsley

In a large skillet heat 2 tablespoons oil. Season the chicken pieces with garlic salt and pepper and sauté for a few minutes until it they start to brown on each side. Add remaining oil and red and yellow peppers and cook for another minute or two. Add garlic and marjoram and cook for 30 seconds, stirring constantly. Add wine and broth and bring to a boil. Add cream simmer for a few minutes until the sauce starts to thicken a bit. Stir in sundried tomatoes and pasta and toss to coat. Serve with shredded Parmesan cheese and chopped basil or parsley on top.

Tortellini with Peas and Ham

1 package (9 to 12 ounces) fresh or frozen cheese tortellini

1/4 cup dry white wine

2 tablespoons butter

2 garlic cloves, minced

1 cup diced ham

1 cup heavy cream

Pinch of nutmeg

1/4 cup parmesan cheese, freshly grated

3/4 cup frozen baby peas, thawed

Salt and pepper

1/2 cup shredded Parmesan cheese

2 tablespoons fresh chopped Italian parsley

Cook tortellini according to package directions. Melt butter in skillet and cook garlic for 30 seconds, stirring constantly. Add heavy cream and wine and bring to a simmer for a few minutes until it starts to thicken a bit. Whisk in cheese and nutmeg. Stir in tortellini, peas and ham and toss to coat. Season to taste with salt and freshly ground black pepper. Serve with a little shredded Parmesan cheese and parsley on top.

Cajun Fettuccini

2 boneless, skinless chicken breast halves, cut into 1 to 2 inch pieces

8 ounces of smoked sausage, diced

1 to 2 tablespoons of Cajun seasoning

2 tablespoons butter

2 tablespoons olive oil

half a red onion, sliced thin

1 red pepper, sliced in thin strips

1 green pepper sliced in thin strips

2 cloves garlic, minced

Salt and pepper

1/2 cup chicken broth

1 to 1½ cups heavy cream

Dash hot sauce (optional)

1 box (16 ounces) fettuccini, cooked al dente

2 tablespoons chopped scallions or Italian parsley

Sprinkle chicken with a little Cajun seasoning. Toss to coat. In a large skillet over medium heat, cook the chicken in butter for a few minutes until it starts to get brown. Add sausage and continue to cook for a few minutes until chicken is cooked through. Remove chicken and sausage to a plate. Add oil to the same skillet. Cook onions and peppers until they start to get a little soft. Season with a little salt and pepper. Add garlic. Cook another 30 seconds, stirring constantly. Add chicken and sausage back to the skillet. Add broth and turn up the heat. Simmer a few minutes. Add 1 cup heavy cream and some more Cajun seasoning if you want and a dash or two of hot sauce. Add pasta and toss. Serve with chopped scallions or parsley on top.

Shrimp Fettuccini Alfredo

1 pint of heavy cream

1 stick or 8 tablespoons of butter

1½ cups fresh grated Parmesan cheese

1/2 teaspoon fresh ground black pepper

1/4 pound of uncooked medium sized shrimp, peeled and deveined

2 to 3 tablespoons chopped scallions or Italian parsley

1 box (16 ounces) hot cooked fetticcini

In a sauce pan heat the cream. Don't boil it! Add the butter. When the butter is melted, whisk in cheese and pepper until smooth. Stir in shrimp and continue to cook on low for a minute or two until the shrimp turns pink. Serve sauce over hot pasta with scallions or parsley on top.

෴ ෴ ෴

I think this is one of the best and easiest fettuccini alfredo recipes ever! Don't want to do the shrimp, leave it out! It's still great without it. Packers' wife Andrea Collins made this for me at my house. We couldn't stop eating it! It's Ireland's favorite. Now she can even make it herself!

෴ ෴ ෴

Linguini with Clam Sauce

1 stick or 8 tablespoons of butter

3 tablespoons of olive oil

3 to 4 cloves garlic, minced

1/2 cup dry white wine or chicken stock

Pinch of red pepper flakes

2 cans (6.5 ounces) minced clams with juice

1 box (16 ounces) linguini, cooked al dente

Salt and pepper

2 tablespoons chopped Italian parsley

Heat butter and oil in a large skillet. Add garlic and red pepper flakes and sauté for 30 seconds, stirring constantly. Add wine and clams with juice. Bring to a simmer. Add pasta. Toss pasta to coat with sauce. Season with a little salt and pepper. Serve with chopped parsley on top.

❧ ❧ ❧

So you're broke, the priest is coming over for dinner and he loves seafood, what do you do? Make this! I love this recipe because it's dirt cheap and super quick and easy to make. When my son Riley was born (wow, that was a long time ago, he's a teenager now) we needed to get him baptized. We invited the priest over for dinner. I heard through the grapevine that he loved seafood. Well, guess what! He loved it! Serve this with a salad some bread, and maybe a dessert and it tastes like a million bucks but only costs you about ten bucks for the whole meal! LOVE THAT!

❧ ❧ ❧

Spaghetti Carbonara

1 box (16 ounces) spaghetti, cooked al dente

1/2 cup heavy cream

4 eggs

1/2 pound bacon, cut into 1/2 inch pieces

1 tablespoon olive oil

2 tablespoons chopped Italian parsley

Salt and black pepper

1 cup freshly grated parmesan cheese, divided

Add the diced bacon to a large skillet. Cook slowly over medium-low heat for about 10 minutes or until crisp. Remove bacon from pan and drain on paper towels. In a large bowl whisk together the eggs, 3/4 cup cheese, heavy cream and olive oil. Drain the hot cooked pasta and toss immediately with the egg mixture. Toss in the cooked bacon and parsley. Season with a little salt and pepper. Serve right away, with the extra grated cheese on top.

᠄ᠥ ᠄ᠥ ᠄ᠥ

Got bacon, eggs, a box of spaghetti, a touch of cream and some parmesan cheese. If so, you've got a super quick and delicious dinner. This one is dirt cheap to make too! It would cost you more than 15 bucks a person for this dish out at a restaurant but it's so easy to make at home! It's kid friendly too! Try it!

᠄ᠥ ᠄ᠥ ᠄ᠥ

Spaghetti with Olive Oil and Garlic

3 to 4 cloves of fresh garlic, minced

1/2 teaspoon of red pepper flakes (optional)

1/2 cup olive oil

1/4 cup chopped Italian parsley

1 box (16 ounces) spaghetti, cooked al dente

1/4 cup grated Parmesan cheese

Drain pasta in a colander, reserving 2 tablespoons of the pasta water. Do not rinse pasta with water. In a large sauté pan, heat olive oil over medium heat. Add the garlic and sauté for about 30 seconds, stirring constantly. Add the red pepper flakes and sauté for another few seconds. Add the reserved pasta water and spaghetti and cook for another 1 minute. Toss in parsley and Parmesan cheese.

Need dinner in like 10 minutes? This is it! It's another super quick, easy, and cheap recipe. My kids love it! I do too. I LOVE pasta! Any kind!

WHAT'S ON THE SIDE?

Bob's Favorite Cheesy Broccoli Bake

4 tablespoons butter, divided

1/2 cup onion, finely diced

2 packages (10 ounces) chopped frozen broccoli, thawed

1 can (10.75 ounces) condensed cream of celery soup

1/4 cup milk

3 cups shredded sharp cheddar cheese, divided

1 cup mayonnaise

2 eggs, beaten

1/2 teaspoon garlic salt

1/4 teaspoon ground black pepper

1½ teaspoons lemon juice

12 to 16 buttery round crackers, crushed

Preheat oven to 350 degrees. Melt 2 tablespoons butter in a skillet over medium heat. Sauté onion until soft. In a bowl, whisk together soup, onions, milk, eggs, mayonnaise, seasonings, and lemon juice. Stir in 1 cup of cheese and all the broccoli. Spray a 2 quart casserole dish with cooking spray. Spoon broccoli mixture into dish. Top with the rest of the cheese and crushed crackers. Then dot the top with the remaining butter. Bake uncovered for 30 to 40 minutes until bubbly and golden on top.

Bacon Wrapped Green Bean Bundles

2 cans (14.5 ounces) whole green beans, drained

1 pound thick sliced bacon

1/2 cup brown sugar

1½ cups of bottled Catalina salad dressing

Plain wooden toothpicks

Bundle about 6 green beans together and wrap with a half slice of bacon. Secure them with a toothpick. Make several bundles and place in a 9" × 13" baking dish. Mix brown sugar and dressing and pour sauce over the beans. Bake uncovered in a preheated 350 degrees for 20 to 35 minutes until the bacon gets a little crispy.

∾ ∾ ∾

This is one of those great southern recipes! Packers' wife Candy Clifton made these for me at my house and I've been making them ever since. They are AMAZING! Especially with the fried chicken recipe in the "What's for Dinner? I'm Hungry!" chapter. Thanks Candy!

∾ ∾ ∾

Jazzed Up Baked Beans

6 to 8 slices of bacon

2 cans (28 ounces) baked beans

1/4 cup onion, finely diced

2 tablespoons Dijon mustard

1 cup ketchup

1 tablespoon apple cider vinegar

1 cup packed brown sugar

Preheat the oven to 350 degrees. Partially cook bacon. Stir together the baked beans, onion, mustard, ketchup, vinegar, and brown sugar. Place in a large casserole dish that has been sprayed with cooking spray. Top with slices of bacon. Bake uncovered for 45 minutes in the preheated oven, until the bacon is crisp and beans are bubbling hot.

       ಌ ಌ ಌ

I'm a big fan of "jazzing things up!" Make canned beans taste like homemade with stuff you already have in your fridge or pantry anyway! Love that bacon on top! These are a hit at all our backyard BBQ's!

       ಌ ಌ ಌ

Pan Roasted Brussels Sprouts

4 slices of bacon, thick-cut

2 tablespoons butter

1 bag (16 ounces) frozen Brussels sprouts, defrosted and halved

1/2 cup onion, finely diced

Salt and pepper

In a large skillet, cook bacon over medium-high heat until crispy. Remove to a paper towel-lined plate and crumble. In same pan you cooked the bacon in melt the butter with the bacon drippings. Add onions and sprouts and cook, stirring occasionally, for about 8 to 10 minutes. Season with salt and pepper and toss the bacon back into pan. Serve right away.

∾ ∾ ∾

So you say you don't like brussels sprouts? Then, you haven't tried these. They are just wonderful! They even won, best side dish in a holiday recipe contest we had on the show. And, let me tell you there was some tough competition, but these won hands down! Thanks Patrick!

∾ ∾ ∾

Cheesy Corn Stuffed Tomatoes

6 to 8 ripe, medium sized tomatoes

4 tablespoons butter, divided

1/4 cup finely diced onion

1/4 cup finely diced green pepper

2½ cups fresh corn kernels

2 tablespoons water

1 tablespoon fresh thyme leaves, or 1/4 teaspoon dried thyme

6 slices bacon, cooked and crumbled

4 tablespoons mayonnaise

1½ cups shredded Muenster or Monterey Jack cheese

3/4 cup fresh breadcrumbs

2 tablespoons fresh chopped Italian parsley

Slice the tops off the tomatoes. Carefully scoop out pulp, leaving a shell. Turn tomatoes upside down and drain on paper towels. Preheat the oven to 400 degrees. Sauté onion and pepper in 1 tablespoon butter until soft. Add water, thyme and corn. Bring to a boil. Cover and cook for 2 to 3 minutes. Season with a little salt and pepper. Turn off heat and stir in bacon and mayonnaise. Season the inside of each tomato with a little salt. Fill each tomato with some of the corn mixture. Melt remaining 3 tablespoons butter. In a small bowl, toss together crumbs, cheese, butter and parsley. Top each tomato with some of the crumb mixture. Bake tomatoes in a foil lined pan for 15 to 25 minutes. You can also broil the tomatoes for a minute after they bake just to brown the tops a bit.

Perfect Mashed Potatoes

289

8 to 10 red potatoes, quartered or 5 to 7 russet or Yukon gold potatoes, peeled and cut into 2" chunks

1 teaspoon salt

1 teaspoon garlic salt

Black pepper

2 to 3 tablespoons butter, plus more for the top

1/4 to 1/2 cup hot milk

Chopped chives or Italian parsley

In a large pan, place potatoes with enough water to cover, and teaspoon of salt, bring to a boil. Simmer for 20 to 30 minutes or until potatoes are really tender when pierced with a fork. Remove from heat and drain potatoes in a colander. Return potatoes to pan. Mash potatoes with a potato masher. Don't use a mixer. Mix in butter, garlic salt, stock and 1/4 cup hot milk. Add extra milk, a little at a time if you need to. Season to taste with extra salt and pepper if desired. Serve with more butter, and chives or parsley on top.

∽ ∽ ∽

Ever had sticky, gluey mashed potatoes? Mine used to be that way. Not anymore! Use this recipe and they turn out perfect every time!

∽ ∽ ∽

Roasted Garlic Mashers

1 whole head of garlic

1 tablespoon olive oil

Piece of foil

5 to 7 russet or Yukon gold potatoes, peeled and cut into 2 inch chunks

1½ teaspoons salt, divided

Freshly ground black or white pepper

2 tablespoons butter, plus more for the top

1/4 to 1/2 cup warm milk or heavy cream

Chopped chives or Italian parsley

To roast garlic, cut off the top (stem end) of the head of garlic. Place the garlic in a piece of foil and drizzle with the olive oil. Wrap tightly and roast in a preheated 375 degree oven for about 45 to 55 minutes until it's completely soft and caramelized. Let cool slightly, then squeeze it into a small bowl and roughly mash. Fill a large pan with water. Add potatoes and 1 teaspoon of the salt, bring to a boil. Reduce heat to medium, cover and cook 20 to 30 minutes or until potatoes are really tender when pierced with a fork. Remove from heat and drain potatoes in colander. Return potatoes to the pan. Mash potatoes with a potato masher. Stir in butter, mashed garlic, remaining 1/2 teaspoon salt and 1/4 cup of milk or cream. Add extra milk or cream, a little at a time, if necessary, for desired consistency. Season with a little extra salt and pepper if they need it. Serve with more butter and chives or parsley on top.

Cheesy Ranch Potatoes

8 medium sized potatoes

1/4 to 1/2 cup milk

1 cup sour cream

1 cup prepared ranch dressing

1/2 cup bacon bits

1 tablespoon dried parsley

4 to 5 cups shredded cheddar cheese

2 cups crushed corn flakes

1/4 cup butter, melted

Peel and boil potatoes until they are fork tender and easy to mash. Drain water. Mash potatoes with 1/4 cup milk, sour cream, and dressing. If too they seem really thick, add a bit more milk. Stir in bacon, parsley and 1 cup of cheese. Place potatoes in a 9" × 13" pan that has been sprayed with cooking spray. Top with rest of cheese. Combine corn flakes and butter, sprinkle over casserole. Bake at 350 degrees for 40 to 55 minutes until brown and bubbly.

∾ ∾ ∾

My kids love these! Me too! Anything with "ranch" in it! Grilling steaks or making a meatloaf? These are the perfect side. Plus, you can totally make them ahead of time. Even up to 3 days! LOVE THAT!

∾ ∾ ∾

Cheesy Green Chili Potatoes

1 bag (32 ounces) southern style, cubed frozen hash browns, slightly thawed

1/2 teaspoon pepper

1 teaspoon garlic salt

2 cups sour cream

2 cans (4 ounces) diced green chilies

1/4 cup diced jalapeno peppers (optional)

1 can (10.75 ounces) cream of celery soup

1½ cups milk

1/4 cup onion, finely diced

5 cups sharp shredded cheddar cheese

2 cups crushed cornflakes

1/4 melted butter

Spray a 9" × 13" pan with cooking spray. In a large bowl, mix together milk, soup, onion, green chilies, jalapenos, garlic salt, pepper and sour cream. Mix in potatoes and 2 cups cheese. Spread mixture in the pan. Sprinkle with remaining 3 cups cheese and top with cornflakes. Drizzle melted butter over the top. Bake covered loosely with foil in a preheated 350 degree oven for 40 to 50 minutes. Uncover and bake another 10 to 20 minutes until bubbly and the top is golden brown.

Fancy Baked Potatoes

4 large baking potatoes

6 tablespoons butter, melted

3 tablespoons grated Parmesan cheese

1 teaspoon salt

1/2 teaspoon pepper

1/2 cup shredded Cheddar cheese (optional)

1/4 cup real bacon bits (optional)

1 scallion, chopped (optional)

Scrub the potatoes. Make several slices in the potatoes but don't cut all the way through, leaving slices attached at the bottom. Place potatoes in a foil lined pan that's been sprayed with cooking spray. Fan out the potato slices a bit with your hands and drizzle butter over the potatoes and in between the slices. Combine the Parmesan cheese, salt and pepper and sprinkle over potatoes and in between the slices. Bake in a preheated 325 degree oven for 40 to 55 minutes or until potatoes are tender. If you want to you can load them up with cheddar cheese, bacon and scallions and bake then for another 5 to 10 minutes or until cheese is melted. You can also wrap these potatoes in foil and grill them for 40 to 55 minutes until they're tender.

Door County Sausage & Cherry Stuffing

1 pound bulk pork sausage

2 tablespoons of butter

3/4 cup finely diced onion

1/2 cup finely chopped celery

1/2 cup dried cherries

2 bags (12 ounces) seasoned stuffing mix, cubes

4 to 5 cups chicken stock

1 tablespoon poultry seasoning

2 tablespoons chopped fresh Italian parsley

Salt and pepper to taste

Brown sausage in large pan. Cook until it's no longer pink and crumbly. Remove the sausage from the pan and set aside. Darin any grease. In the same pan cook onion and celery in the butter until soft. Remove from the heat and add cherries, poultry seasoning and parsley. Add a little salt and pepper. Add sausage and stuffing cubes and toss to mix. Slowly add stock and mix until moistened but not soggy.   Place in a large casserole dish that has been sprayed with cooking spray. Cover with foil and bake in a preheated 350 degree oven for 25 minutes. Remove foil and bake another 15 to 20 minutes to crisp up the top a bit.

∾ ∾ ∾

A lovely gal who lives in Door County made this on my show. I've been making it ever since. We love Door County cherries! And, Michigan cherries too!

∾ ∾ ∾

Slow Cooker Stuffing

1 stick of butter

2 cups chopped onion

2 cups chopped celery

1/4 cup finely chopped Italian parsley

8 ounces fresh sliced mushrooms (optional)

1 bag (16 ounces) stuffing cubes

2 teaspoons poultry seasoning

2 to 4 cups chicken stock

Melt butter in skillet and sauté onion and celery. Pour over bread cubes in a very large bowl. Add mushrooms, parsley and poultry seasoning and stir well. Pour in 2 or more cups chicken stock to moisten. Pack lightly into a slow cooker that has been sprayed with cooking spray. Cover and cook on low 2 to 3 hours. Stir often. Watch so it doesn›t burn. If too dry, add more stock.

෴ ෴ ෴

I never thought of doing stuffing in the slow cooker until I met my friend Arlene. Great idea, because it free up your oven! Especially during the holidays when not one more thing can fit in there!

෴ ෴ ෴

Simply Wonderful Stuffing for Seafood

1 tablespoon olive oil

8 to 12 tablespoons of butter, melted

1/2 cup onion, finely diced

1/4 cup celery, finely diced

1/4 red pepper, finely diced

1 (6 ounce) can lump crabmeat, drained

1 tablespoon dry white wine (optional)

1 tablespoon fresh lemon juice

2 teaspoons old bay seasoning salt

Half pound or 2 sleeves buttery crackers, crushed

2 tablespoons minced parsley

In a skillet cook onions, celery, and red pepper in the oil until they just start to get soft. Put the crackers, cooked vegetables, wine, parsley, Old Bay, lemon juice, and crab in a big bowl. Drizzle 8 tablespoons of the butter over the top and mix well. If too it seems a little too dry add a little more melted butter, wine or even just a teaspoon or two of water. Stuff this in butterflied shrimp, lobster tails, or great on haddock or other, white flaky fish. Drizzle with a little more butter if you want and sprinkle with a little paprika and bake until seafood is done and stuffing is a little browned on top.

∾ ∾ ∾

This stuff really is buttery and WONDERFUL! You don't eat this as a side. Instead it's meant to go on top of seafood before you make it. Stuff lobster with some or shrimp, or spoon it on fish fillets before baking. WOW! Talk about a great date night!

∾ ∾ ∾

Roasted Acorn Squash

1 acorn squash

4 tablespoons butter

4 tablespoons brown sugar

salt and pepper

2 pieces of foil

Preheat the oven to 350 degrees. Carefully cut the acorn squash in half. Scoop out seeds and stringy insides. Season the squash with a little salt and pepper. Take 2 pieces of foil and roll them up. Next, fold each piece to make a circle. Flatten the circles a bit and put them it in a baking dish. Set squash halves cut side up on top of foil. This keeps the squash from touching the bottom of the pan. Place 2 tablespoons butter and 2 tablespoons brown sugar in each half. Bake for 50 to 60 minutes until squash flesh is soft. Serve warm. Serves two but you can double or triple the recipe if you need to serve more people.

૦૦ ૦૦ ૦૦

Bob LOVES acorn squash! I admit it, I don't make it enough. These are just so yummy and easy too. I love to serve them with pork and wild rice in the fall!

૦૦ ૦૦ ૦૦

Fresh Cranberry Sauce

1 cup water

1 cup sugar

1 bag (12 ounces) fresh cranberries

Pinch of cinnamon (optional)

2 tablespoons fresh orange juice

2 teaspoons fresh orange zest

In a medium saucepan, combine water sugar and cranberries. Bring to a boil and simmer for about 10 minutes until the skins pop, stirring occasionally. Taste to see if it's sweet enough for you, If not add a little more sugar and water if needed and cook a minute or two longer. Stir in orange juice and cinnamon and cook a minute or so. Remove from the heat and stir in orange zest. Serve warm or chilled.

ে০ ে০ ে০

I grew up with the cranberry stuff that comes out shaped like the can. I never liked it much. Now, every Thanksgiving Ireland and I make fresh cranberry sauce. We both love it! Add some of the leftover sauce to plain cream cheese. It makes a great spread on bagels!

ে০ ে০ ে০

Cornbread with Honey Butter

1 cup softened butter

1/4 to 1/2 cup honey

1½ cups cornmeal

2 cups buttermilk

1/2 cup milk

2 cups all-purpose flour

1 tablespoon baking powder

1 teaspoon salt

1/2 cup sugar

2 eggs

1/2 cup vegetable oil

Preheat the oven to 350 degrees. In a small bowl, mix butter and honey until smooth. Set aside until ready to use. In another bowl, combine cornmeal, buttermilk and milk. Let stand for 5 minutes. Spray a 9" × 13" baking pan with cooking spray. In a large bowl, mix together flour, baking powder, salt and sugar. Mix in the cornmeal mixture, eggs and oil until smooth. Spoon the batter into the pan. Bake for 30 to 35 minutes, or until a knife inserted into the center of the cornbread comes out clean. Serve warm with honey butter.

∾ ∾ ∾

I didn't have one of those little blue boxes and wanted corn bread one day so I came up with this recipe. I love it because it makes a nice, big batch!

∾ ∾ ∾

Beer Bread

3 cups self-rising flour

1/4 cup sugar

1 bottle (12 ounces) of beer

1/2 cup melted butter

Preheat the oven to 375 degrees. Spray a loaf pan with cooking spray. In a large bowl, combine the flour, sugar, and beer. The batter should be really lumpy!!! Don't over mix it! Spoon it into the loaf pan and pour the butter on top. Bake for about 45 minutes or until it gets all golden brown.

∾ ∾ ∾

Need bread for soup or stew? Keep some self-rising flour in the pantry and a couple bottles a beer in the house and you're set. I'm not a baker, so it's gotta be really easy! This is! I got this recipe for a great gal named Jenn. She made it on my show. She mixes the flour and sugar together and puts it in canning jars. She gives it as gifts with directions attached to add the beer and butter. Great idea Jenn! Homemade beer bread mixes, and they cost just a few cents each! LOVE THAT!

∾ ∾ ∾

DANGEROUSLY EASY BUT DELICIOUS DESSERTS

All-American Berry Trifle

1 angel food cake cut in 1 to 2 inch cubes

2 packages (3.4 ounces) instant vanilla or French vanilla pudding

2½ cups cold milk

1 container (12 ounces) frozen whipped topping, thawed

4 cups assorted fresh berries (raspberries, sliced strawberries, blueberries, blackberries)

Fresh mint sprigs

In a large bowl, beat the milk and pudding mixes together until pudding starts to thicken. Fold about 3/4 of the whopped topping into the pudding mixture. In another bowl gently toss berries together. Layer half of the cake into the bottom of a trifle dish or clear glass bowl. Next, spoon half of the pudding mixture on top of the cake. Then, spoon about 1/3 of the berries on top of the pudding. Repeat. Next, spread remaining whipped topping on top. Let refrigerate a few hours before serving. Before serving, top with remaining berries and fresh mint.

∾ ∾ ∾

I love to cook, but I'm just not a baker! Never have been! I just don't have the time or the patience! That's why I started making trifles! I bought a cheap pretty trifle dish. (I think I paid less then ten bucks for it.) Now, when I need to serve or bring a dessert that will really WOW 'em. It's a no brainer! I make a trifle. This is one of my favorites, especially on those holiday weekends in the summer. It looks so pretty! And, they are so easy! Another "Rock Star" moment! LOVE THOSE!

∾ ∾ ∾

Chocolate Raspberry Trifle

1 pan (9" × 13") of your favorite brownies, prepared and cooled

2 packages (3.4 ounces) instant chocolate pudding

2½ cups cold milk

1 container (12 ounces) frozen whipped topping, thawed

2 cups fresh raspberries

3/4 teaspoon cornstarch

3 tablespoons sugar

2 tablespoons water

1 dark chocolate bar

Fresh mint sprigs

Cut brownies into small bite size squares. In a large bowl, beat the milk and pudding mixes together until pudding starts to thicken. Fold about 3/4 of the whipped topping into the pudding mixture using a spatula. In a saucepan, heat all but a handful of berries, sugar, cornstarch and water. Stir for a few minutes on low. Let cool. Layer half of the brownies into the bottom of a trifle dish or clear glass bowl. Spoon half of the raspberry sauce on top of brownies. Next, spoon half of the pudding mixture on top. Repeat. Spread remaining whipped topping on top. Cover with plastic wrap and refrigerate until ready to serve. Use a vegetable peeler to make chocolate shavings with the chocolate bar. Sprinkle shavings on the top along with remaining fresh berries and mint.

ᏑᎾ ᏑᎾ ᏑᎾ

Here's another AMAZING trifle for you! This one is great for Valentine's or Mother's Day! I love the combination of raspberries and chocolate!!

ᏑᎾ ᏑᎾ ᏑᎾ

Chocolate Peppermint Trifle

1 package chocolate cake mix, baked in a 9" × 13" pan, according to package directions

4 cups cold milk

2 packages (3.4 ounces) chocolate instant pudding

1 container (12 ounces) whipped topping, thawed

2 cups crushed peppermint candy or candy canes

Fresh mint sprigs

Cool cake and cut into 1/2" cubes. Add milk to dry pudding mix in medium bowl. Beat until pudding starts to thicken. Layer half each of cake cubes, pudding, whipping topping and peppermint candy in large glass trifle bowl. Repeat all layers, leaving some of the whipped topping and peppermint candy to decorate the top.

∾ ∾ ∾

Here's a fun trifle for the holidays! Great for a holiday party! The kids LOVE it! Seems like we always have lots of broken candy canes around!

∾ ∾ ∾

My Family's Favorite Chocolate Chip Cookies

2¼ cups flour

1 teaspoon salt

1 teaspoon baking soda

1 stick margarine, softened

1 stick butter, softened

1 cup brown sugar

1/2 cup granulated sugar

2 large eggs

1 teaspoon vanilla extract

1 tablespoon water

1 bag semi-sweet chocolate chips

Heat oven to 325 degrees. Mix flour, salt, and baking soda together in medium bowl, set aside. With an electric mixer, mix butter, margarine, and sugars until thoroughly blended and fluffy. Mix in eggs, water, and vanilla. Gradually add dry ingredients, mix until just combined. Stir in chips. Drop spoonfuls of dough on a cookie sheet lined with parchment paper. Bake, reversing cookie sheets positions halfway through baking, until cookies are light, golden brown (about 8 to 15 minutes start checking at 5 minutes). Let cookies cool for a few minutes on cookie sheets before serving.

❧ ❧ ❧

Okay, so I do bake every once in awhile! This is our very favorite cookie recipe. Yep, I do let the kids nibble on just a little of the dough and lick the beaters too! That's the stuff I hope they remember!

❧ ❧ ❧

Super Easy Peanut Butter Cookies

1 cup peanut butter

1 cup sugar

1 egg

Beat all the ingredients together. Drop onto baking sheets. Press down a bit with a fork. Bake in a preheated 350 degrees oven 10 to 15 minutes. Cool about ten minutes before eating

∾ ∾ ∾

Craving cookies? You can whip these up in 15 minutes. Just make sure to use the regular peanut butter. These are perfect on a snow day when the kids are home from school and you have no idea what to do with them all day. Been there!

∾ ∾ ∾

Cherry Dump Cake

2 cans (21 ounces) cherry pie filling

1 package (18.25 ounces) yellow cake mix

1 stick of butter, melted

1½ cups chopped pecans (optional)

Spray a 9" × 13" pan with cooking spray. Dump the 2 cans of cherry pie filling into the bottom of the pan. Sprinkle the box of cake mix evenly on top of that. Drizzle butter on top of the cake mix. Spread pecans evenly over the butter and cake mix. Bake in a preheated, 350 degree oven for 30 to 45 minutes and serve warm. This is delicious with a scoop of vanilla ice cream.

∾ ∾ ∾

Just too easy! My dad LOVES cherry pie! This is so much easier. You MUST serve this warm. You can use skip the nuts and use a chocolate cake mix too. Then you've got kind of a black forest dessert going on. I always keep lots of boxed cake mixes on hand, and canned frosting too just in case! "Mom, I need to bring cupcakes to school tomorrow." No problem, I got it covered!

∾ ∾ ∾

Peach Pecan Dump Cake

2 cans (28 ounces) sliced peaches in heavy syrup, undrained

1 package (18.25 ounces) yellow cake mix

1 stick of butter, melted

1½ cups chopped pecans

1½ cups flaked coconut

In the bottom of an unsprayed 9" × 13" baking pan, pour in peaches and syrup. Cover with dry cake mix; drizzle butter over the top. Sprinkle with pecans and coconut. Bake uncovered, at 350 degrees for 30 to 35 minutes.

෨ ෨ ෨

I'm all about any recipe that has the word "DUMP" in it. Thanks to Lonnie for this one! I love the coconut in this one, but if you don't leave it out!

෨ ෨ ෨

Death by Chocolate Cake

1 package (18.25 ounces) devil's food cake mix

1 packages (5.9 ounces) instant chocolate pudding mix

1 cup sour cream

3/4 cup vegetable oil

4 eggs

1/2 cup warm water

2 cups semi-sweet chocolate chips

Powdered sugar

Whipped cream (optional)

Fresh raspberries or strawberries (optional)

Preheat oven to 350 degrees. In a large bowl, mix together the cake and pudding mix, sour cream, oil, eggs and water. Stir in the chocolate chips and pour batter into a bundt pan that has been sprayed with cooking spray. Bake for 50 to 55 minutes, or until top is springy to the touch and a wooden toothpick inserted comes out clean. Cool cake thoroughly in pan at least an hour and a half before putting on a plate, dust the cake with powdered sugar. Serve with fresh whipped cream and a few raspberries or strawberries on the side.

ଏ ଏ ଏ

Okay, I admit it. I am a serious chocoholic!! It's not my fault! My mom is too! Blame it on her! This recipe is a great way to jazz up an ordinary chocolate cake mix! So go find, borrow, or buy a bundt pan! They look so pretty and no frosting needed! LOVE THAT!

ଏ ଏ ଏ

Root Beer Float Cake

1 package (18.25 ounces) white cake mix

1¼ cup root beer

2 eggs

1/4 cup vegetable oil

Frosting:

2 packets (1.3 ounces) Dream Whip whipped topping

1 cup chilled root beer

Crushed root beer barrel candies

In a mixing bowl, combine the first four cake ingredients. Beat on low speed for 30 seconds. Beat on high for 2 minutes. Pour into greased 9" × 13" baking pan. Bake at 350 degrees for 25 to 40 minutes or until toothpick inserted into center comes out clean. Cool completely. In another bowl, beat frosting ingredients until stiff peaks form. Frost cake. Chill. When ready to serve, sprinkle root beer candies on top.

When is the last time you had a root beer float? I used to love 'em. Actually, I still do! That's why this cake is so fun! Tastes just like one. The recipe comes from a gal from Sturgeon Bay. She made it on my show in a summer recipe contest. It won first place in the desserts category. Thanks Tracie!

Lemon Poppy Seed Cake

1 package (18.25 ounces) lemon cake mix

4 eggs

1/2 cup vegetable oil

1 package (3.4 ounces) instant lemon pudding mix

1 cup lemon-lime soda or water

1/4 cup poppy seeds

Preheat oven to 350 degrees. Grease and flour a bundt pan. You can also use 2, 8" × 4" loaf pans or 4 to 5 mini loaf pans. In a large bowl, mix together the cake mix, eggs, oil, pudding mix, water, and poppy seeds. Spread batter into pans. Bake for 30 to 35 minutes or until a toothpick inserted into the cake comes out clean.

൭ ൭ ൭

I love a good lemon poppy seed cake and this is one! It's a great recipe because you can make one big cake, a couple loaves of lemon poppy seed bread, or mini loaves too. Welcome a new neighbor with a loaf! This recipe is great for bake sales! You can make lots of mini loaves. I have a pan that you can that bakes 4 mini loaves in at one time. It's so cool!

൭ ൭ ൭

~ ~ ~

Ireland and a few of her Girl Scout friends at a bake sale. They do lots of bake sales to raise money for special trips and activities. One time I did 12 dozen cupcakes. I'll never forget that night! Frosting everywhere! Next time I'm doing the lemon poppy seed mini loaves! Way easier!

~ ~ ~

The Kid's Favorite Oreo Torte

1 package (20 ounces) Oreo cookies

1 stick butter, melted

1 package (8 ounces) cream cheese, softened

1 container (16 ounces) frozen whipped topping, thawed and divided

1/4 cup powdered sugar

2¼ cups cold milk, divided

1 cup heavy cream

1 small box instant chocolate pudding

1 small box instant vanilla pudding

Finely crush all but 5 or 6 Oreos. Mix crushed cookies with butter and press into bottom of 9" × 13" pan. In one large bowl, beat both puddings with 2 cups milk. Add heavy cream and beat until pudding starts to thicken. In another bowl, beat together softened cream cheese, 1/4 cup milk and powdered sugar until smooth. Mix in half of the container of cool whip. Spread the cream cheese mixture on top of cookie crust. Next, spoon pudding mixture on top of cream cheese layer. Then carefully spread remaining whipped topping on top of the pudding. Crumble the remaining cookies on top of the whipped topping. Cover and refrigerate for at least 2 hours before serving.

∾ ∾ ∾

My friend Annette, (if I'm "The Queen of Casseroles", then she's the "Queen of Desserts") brought this to a dinner at our house one night and the kids went crazy over it. Riley wants me to make it now every year on his birthday. Gee, thanks Annette!! Oh well, at least it's easy!

∾ ∾ ∾

Bob's Favorite Chocolate Torte

1 stick butter

1¼ cups all-purpose flour

3/4 cup finely-chopped pecans

2 packages (8 ounces) softened cream cheese

1 cup powdered sugar

1 container (16 ounces) frozen whipped topping, thawed

3½ cups milk

2 boxes (3.4 ounces) instant chocolate pudding

1 chocolate candy bar

With a fork or pastry blender mix together butter, flour, and pecans. Press into a 9" × 13" pan. Bake for approximately 10 minutes in a preheated, 350 degree oven until light golden brown. Remove from oven and let cool. In a medium mixing bowl beat together powdered sugar and softened cream cheese. Fold in half of the container of whipped topping. Spread the mixture over the cooled crust. Beat milk and two packages pudding mix together until it starts to thicken a bit. Spread over cream cheese layer. Spread the other half of the whipped topping over pudding layer. Use a vegetable peeler to make chocolate shavings with the candy bar. Sprinkle them on top of dessert. Refrigerate several hours or overnight until ready to serve.

∾ ∾ ∾

Another reason why Bob married me. I got a hold of a pie recipe his mom used to make for him as a kid. I doubled the recipe it turned into this torte. It's really rich, so just a little piece will do ya. I don't make it often but when I do, He loves it!

∾ ∾ ∾

My Favorite Pistachio Torte

1½ cups flour

3/4 cup butter

1/4 cup pecans, finely chopped

2 tablespoons sugar

1 package (8 ounces) cream cheese, softened

1 package (16 ounces) frozen whipped topping, thawed

1/2 cup powdered sugar

2 packages (3 ounces) instant pistachio pudding mix

3½ cups milk

For the crust, combine flour, butter, nuts and sugar and press into a 9" × 13" pan and bake in a preheated 350 degree oven for 8 to 15 minutes. Do not let it brown. Let Cool. Beat together cream cheese, 1/2 carton whipped topping, and powdered sugar and spread on crust. In another bowl, mix pudding mix and milk for 2 minutes. Then spread on top. Top with remaining whipped topping. Refrigerate at least 4 hours before serving.

∽ ∽ ∽

Here's another great torte. LOVE, LOVE, LOVE pistachio pudding. Nobody ever makes it any more. By the way we love our tortes in Wisconsin! Those, creamy, wonderful layered desserts. Got any good torte recipes? I'm always looking for new ones! Email them to me. You can find me on Facebook too.

∽ ∽ ∽

Creamy Coconut Torte

1½ cups all purpose flour

2 tablespoons sugar

3/4 cup butter

1/2 cup finely chopped pecans (optional)

1 package (8 ounces) cream cheese, softened

1 cup powered sugar

1 container (16 ounces) frozen whipped topping, thawed

3½ cups cold milk

3 packages (3.4 ounces) instant coconut cream pudding mix

1 cup flaked coconut, toasted

Preheat oven to 325 degrees. In a medium bowl, combine flour, sugar and butter. Mix until crumbly. Stir in pecans. Spray a 9" × 13" baking dish with cooking spray. Press into dish. Bake for 10 minutes. Cool. In a small mixing bowl, beat the cream cheese and powered sugar until smooth, fold in 1/2 cup of whipped topping. Spread over the crust. In a separate bowl, beat milk and pudding mixes until pudding starts to thicken. Spread over cream cheese mixture. Top with remaining whipped topping. Sprinkle with coconut. Refrigerate at least 4 hours before serving.

～ ～ ～

Here's a fun one for a luau! Or when you're craving a tropical vacation, but it's just not going to happen. Oh well, maybe next year. Until then, have a piece of the torte!

～ ～ ～

Cherry Pretzel Torte

2 cans (20 ounces) cherry pie filling

2 packages (8 ounces) cream cheese, softened

1 container (12 ounces) frozen whipped topping, thawed

1/2 cup powdered sugar

2 cups crushed pretzels (not too finely crushed)

1/2 cup sugar

1 cup melted butter

In a 9" x 13" inch glass pan mix pretzels, butter and sugar together. Press down to form the crust. In a large bowl add cream cheese and powdered sugar. Use a mixer to beat until smooth. Mix in whipped topping. Spoon over the crust. Spread cherries on top. Chill for a few hours before cutting into squares and serving.

෨ ෨ ෨

Pretzels in a dessert! Yep, and it's really good too. No baking either! I got this idea from my friends on the Service League in Oshkosh. It's just yummy!

෨ ෨ ෨

Seven Layer Bars

1½ cups unsalted butter (3 sticks), melted

4½ cups graham cracker crumbs

2 cans (14 ounces) sweetened condensed milk

2½ cups chocolate chips

2½ cups butterscotch chips

1½ cups chopped pecans

1½ cups shredded coconut

Preheat oven to 350 degrees. Place butter in an 11" × 17" baking pan. Melt in oven. Remove pan from oven and carefully tilt pan to spread melted butter around. Sprinkle graham cracker crumbs over melted butter. Toss chips, pecans and coconut together in a big bowl. Pour it over graham cracker crust. Next pour the two cans of condense milk on top. Bake 25 minutes. Cool. Cut into bars.

∾ ∾ ∾

I used to always pick these up at the bakery 'cause I never knew how to make them at home. Well, now I do. Thanks to my friend and pastry chef Lisa. Love this recipe because it makes a big batch!

∾ ∾ ∾

Lemon Bars

Crust:

4½ cups all-purpose flour

1½ cups powdered sugar

1½ cups butter, cubed

Filling Ingredients:

8 large eggs

Zest of 3 lemons

1/2 cup fresh lemon juice (approx. 3 lemons)

3/4 cups all-purpose flour

2 teaspoons baking powder

2 teaspoons salt

4 cups sugar

For the crust:

Coat an 11" × 17" pan with cooking spray. Combine all ingredients in the food processor. Spread crust evenly on the bottom of a sheet pan and press down lightly. Bake at 350 for 8 to 10 minutes.

For the filling:

In a large bowl, use a mixer to mix all ingredients well. Pour them over hot crust. Bake at 350 degrees for 30 to 40 minutes or until it is set in the middle. Chill before cutting into squares.

Cherry Almond Crisp

2 cups pitted fresh or frozen cherries

1/2 cup white sugar

1 teaspoon vanilla extract

1/2 teaspoon almond extract

2 tablespoons flour

1/2 cup old fashion oats

1/2 cup flour

1/2 cup brown sugar

Pinch of cinnamon

1/4 cup butter, melted

In a medium bowl, mix the cherries, extracts, 2 tablespoons flour and white sugar. Evenly distribute the cherry mixture into four buttered ramekins or one buttered 8" × 8" pan. Combine the oats, 1/2 cup flour, brown sugar, cinnamon, baking powder, baking soda and melted butter together. Crumble evenly over the cherry mixture. If you are baking them in ramekins, put them on a cookie sheet. Bake in a preheated 350 degree oven for about 20 to 35 minutes until bubbly and golden on top.

∾ ∾ ∾

I don't do pies much, but I do make crisps. They're way easier! No crust! Thanks to my friend and pastry chef Lindsey for this one. Gotta serve this warm out of the oven with a scoop of vanilla bean ice cream!

∾ ∾ ∾

Triple Berry Crisp

1½ cups blackberries

1½ cups raspberries

1½ cups blueberries

4 tablespoons white sugar

2 cups flour

2 cups rolled oats

1½ cup packed brown sugar

1 teaspoon ground cinnamon

1/2 teaspoon ground nutmeg

1½ cups butter

Vanilla ice cream

Preheat oven to 350 degrees. In a large bowl, gently toss together blackberries, raspberries, blueberries, and white sugar, set aside. In a separate bowl, combine flour, oats, brown sugar, cinnamon and nutmeg. Cut in butter until crumbly. Press half of the mixture in the bottom of a 9" × 13" pan. Cover with berries. Sprinkle remaining crumble mixture over the berries. Bake for 30 to 40 minutes or until fruit is bubbly and topping is golden brown. Serve warm with ice cream.

This is one of my recipes. Told, you I like to make crisps! This makes a nice big one! Perfect way to end a summer party!

Easy Apple Crisp

8 medium apples, peeled and diced

1 cup sugar

1 cup flour

1/2 cup butter

1 teaspoon cinnamon

1 teaspoon apple pie spice

Preheat oven to 400 degrees. In small combine sugar, flour and butter until crumbly. Place peeled, diced apples in a 8" × 8" square baking dish. Sprinkle cinnamon and apple pie over apples and stir. Crumble butter mixture over apples. Bake for 25 to 30 minutes.

෨ ෨ ෨

Pete Petoniak, our chief weather guy at the station always raved about his wife, Sarah's apple crisp. He was right! It's so good! A super simple recipe. Sometimes the simple ones are the best. Again, I like all my crisps best warm out of the oven with a little vanilla ice cream. Thanks Sarah! Love you guys!

෨ ෨ ෨

Easiest Ever Apple Dumplings

2 granny smith apples

2 cans crescent rolls

2 sticks butter

1 cup white sugar

1/2 cup brown sugar

1 teaspoon vanilla

1/2 teaspoon cinnamon

1 mini can of sprite or mountain dew

Peel and core apples. Cut apples into 8 slices each. Sprinkle a little cinnamon over apples. Roll each apple slice in a crescent roll. Place in a 9" × 13" pan that's been sprayed with cooking spray. Melt butter, then add both sugars and stir. Add vanilla, stir and pour over apples. Pour soda around the edges and middle of pan. Sprinkle a little more cinnamon on top and bake at 350 for 30 to 40 minutes or until tops are golden brown. Serve warm with ice cream and spoon some of the sweet sauces from the pan over the top. You can also cut this recipe in half and bake in an 8" × 8" pan.

Okay, now this my kind of recipe! It just doesn't get much easier than this! I think I've told you to always keep a can or two of crescent rolls around? This is why! Craving dessert? Here you go! One of THE BEST and THE EASIEST desserts ever!! Try it! Really!

Easy As Pie Ice Cream Pie

1 small package (3.4 ounces) instant pudding (any flavor)

1 pint vanilla ice cream, softened

1 graham cracker crust

Whipped cream

Beat together pudding mix and ice cream with a mixer. Spread in pie crust. Refrigerate for at least 6 hours or overnight until set. Top with whipped cream.

❧ ❧ ❧

This is Nana, my great-grandmother's recipe. She liked to make it with butterscotch pudding. The kids like it with chocolate. Just make sure you use instant pudding. And, yes you refrigerate it, don't freeze it. (We'll I'm sure you could but she never did.)

❧ ❧ ❧

Triple Chocolate Mess

1 box (18.25 ounces) chocolate cake mix

1 pint sour cream

1 small package (3.5 ounces) instant chocolate pudding

2 cups chocolate chips

3/4 cup oil

4 eggs

1 cup water

Vanilla ice cream

Spray slow cooker with cooking spray. Mix all ingredients in a bowl. Spoon it in to the slow cooker. Cook on low for 1 to 2 hours. It should be a little soupy. Do not overcook! Serve it warm in bowls with vanilla ice cream.

ରେ ରେ ରେ

My friend Susan told me about this recipe. Her mom always makes it for the grandkids. I just had to have it. Whenever the kids invite friends over, I make this. They always want me to give the recipe to their moms so they can make it too, Here it is everybody. A great movie, night treat!!

ରେ ରେ ରେ

Molten Lava Cakes

8 squares (1 ounce) semi-sweet baking chocolate

10 tablespoons butter

1/2 cup all-purpose flour

1½ cups powdered sugar

3 large eggs

3 egg yolks

2 teaspoons vanilla extract

6 (6 ounce) custard cups

Preheat oven to 400 degrees and spray 6 (6 ounce) custard cups with cooking spray. Melt chocolate and butter in a double boiler. Add flour and sugar to chocolate mixture. Stir in eggs until smooth. Stir in vanilla. Divide batter evenly among custard cups. Bake for 12 to 18 minutes. Edges should be firm but the center will be runny. Run a knife around the edge to loosen and invert onto dessert plate.

❧ ❧ ❧

This is one of those fancy restaurant desserts. Guess, what? Now you can make it at home. Hey, if I can do it, you can to. Just invest or borrow some oven safe custard cups. This is so good with fresh raspberries and whipped cream! SERIOUSLY GOOD!

❧ ❧ ❧

Easiest Ever Fudge

1 can (14 ounces) sweetened condensed milk

3 cups chocolate chips (semi-sweet, milk, or a combination)

2 tablespoons butter

1 teaspoon vanilla

1 cup chopped pecans or walnuts, optional

Lightly butter a 9" square pan, line with a piece of plastic wrap, leaving the ends out to cover the finished fudge. The ends will also serve as handles which will help you lift the fudge out of the pan. Heat condensed milk, chocolate chips, butter and vanilla in a double boiler over simmering water. Stir until the chocolate is melted and mixture is smooth. Stir in nuts if you want and pour into the pan. Spread gently then cover lightly with the ends of the plastic wrap. Chill until firm. Lift out of the pan and cut into small squares.

∽ ∽ ∽

My Riley is a "FUDGE NUT"! This recipe is so easy and it turns out just perfect! It also makes a great gift at the holidays.

∽ ∽ ∽

My Dad's Homemade Vanilla Ice Cream

1 cup whole milk

1 cup half and half

2 cups heavy whipping cream

1 cup sugar

1½ teaspoons vanilla extract

Dash salt

Mix together. Put in ice cream maker and follow ice cream machine maker directions. Some machines require ice and rock salt. Best if eaten right away.

∾ ∾ ∾

I was so excited to find this recipe. It was tucked inside Dad's old electric ice cream maker. We plugged the 'ole thing in and guess what? It still works! So, does the recipe. Make some home made ice this summer! Wow, talk about some great memories!

∾ ∾ ∾

Homemade Ice Cream Sandwiches

24 to 30 graham cracker squares

1 container (8 ounces) frozen whipped topping, thawed

1 box (3.4 ounces) instant pudding any flavor (we like chocolate!)

1½ cups cold milk

Sprinkles, nuts, mini M & M's, or mini chocolate chips (optional)

Beat together the pudding and the milk until smooth. Fold in the whipped topping. Place a dollop of the pudding mixture on half of the graham crackers and top with another graham cracker to make a sandwich. Dip the sides in nuts or candies if you want. Wrap each in plastic wrap and freeze for a couple hours if you can wait!

೧ ೧ ೧

Want to be the coolest mom in the neighborhood? Make these! Have the kids over to help. On those summer days when they say "I'm bored" (man would I loved to be bored!) this is a fun thing to do. Make extras! I keep them in big bags in my freezer. Then when it's hot out and the kids want to a cool treat, no problem, I've got 'em.

೧ ೧ ೧

Chocolate Fondue

3/4 to 1 cup heavy cream

2 bags (12 ounces) semisweet chocolate chips

Splash of Kahlua liqueur (optional)

Carefully heat together chocolate chips and the 3/4 cup of the cream until melted. Stir until smooth. Add a splash of liqueur if you want. If it is still a little thick you can add some more cream. Pour chocolate mixture into fondue pot and serve with fresh fruit and other goodies like pound or angel food cake and butter cookies for dipping.

∽ ∽ ∽

We love fondue! It doesn't get much easier than this. And, just wait 'til you bring it out to the table. Talk about ROCK STAR moment!! Come on, do fondue!

∽ ∽ ∽

Orange Cream Pops

1 cup of milk

1 pint of vanilla ice cream

6 ounces of frozen orange juice concentrate, thawed

Small paper cups

Mix all the ingredients in a blender until smooth. Pour into small paper cups. Cover each cup with a small piece of foil and put a popsicle stick in the center. Freeze until firm. Take off foil and peel away cup when ready to eat.

∾ ∾ ∾

My son Riley LOVES popsicles!! It's kind of fun to make your own, especially when the kids are out of school in the summer. That's the time to get them into the kitchen! Start off with fun recipes like homemade popsicles and the next thing you know they'll be wanting to help you make dinner.

∾ ∾ ∾

Ireland and our dog, Levi, hangin' out on a hot summer day. I pass out lots of popsicles in the summer! Make your own some time! It's fun and the kids love 'em!

333

I'M THIRSTY!

Hot Apple Cider

1/2 cup light brown sugar

1 cup orange juice

1 tablespoon orange zest

3 cinnamon sticks

1 gallon apple cider

Whipped cream

Carmel ice cream topping

In a large pot heat first 5 ingredients. Ladle into mugs. Top with whipped cream and drizzle caramel on top.

∾ ∾ ∾

Make a big batch of this in the fall or during the holidays. It's just so good! Love that little bit of orange in there. This is a fun one to make Halloween night for your trick or treaters who usually come home freezing cold! At least in Wisconsin they do!

∾ ∾ ∾

∾ ∾ ∾

Ireland and a friend ready for a fun night of trick or treating. We layer up underneath our costumes here in Wisconsin 'cause it's usually really cold on Halloween night. I've got hot apple cider and a pot of chili on the stove when the kids come home. Got to get something in their stomachs before they start gobbling up the all that candy!

∾ ∾ ∾

Mulled Apple Cranberry Cider

12 cups apple juice

6 cups cranberry juice

1/2 cup brown sugar

2 teaspoons pure vanilla extract

4 cinnamon sticks

4 whole cloves

Combine all of the ingredients together and simmer over low heat for 20 minutes. Serve warm in mugs.

∾ ∾ ∾

I like to serve this during the holidays. It makes the house smell so good! Everybody LOVES it! Take a break from those Christmas cards and all that holiday shopping for some "me" time. You need it! Make some of this and get into a good book. The cards will get out on time, no worries! And, if they don't it's not the end of the world!

∾ ∾ ∾

Mulled Wine

3 bottles (750 milliliter) dry red wine

3 cinnamon sticks

1/4 to 1/2 cup brown sugar

1/2 teaspoon ground cloves

1/4 teaspoon ground nutmeg

2 oranges

1/4 cup brandy

Extra cinnamon sticks for the mugs (optional)

Use a knife or vegetable peeler to zest the orange into thin strips. Then juice the orange into a large heavy pan. Pour in the wine and the orange strips and remaining ingredients. Cover and heat on for about 30 minutes. Be careful not to boil. Serve warm in mugs.

Got a holiday party or a book club? Make this. You don't need to buy expensive wine. Got a big group coming? Just double or triple the recipe. Light a fire in the fireplace or some candles and relax! This is wonderful served with my "Baked Brie with Apples" recipe in the first chapter!

Snowflake Hot Cocoa

2 cups heavy cream

6 cups milk

1 teaspoon vanilla

1 package (12 ounces) white chocolate chips

Whipped cream

Candy canes

Stir together the whipping cream, milk, vanilla and chocolate chips in a slow cooker. Cover and cook on low for 2 to 2½ hours, stirring occasionally, until mixture is hot and chips are melted. Stir again before serving. Garnish with whipped cream and candy canes. You can make this in a large soup pan on the stove. Stir often and heat on low heat for about 20 to 40 minutes. Be careful not to burn.

∽ ∽ ∽

Don't throw out those crushed candy canes. My kids LOVE hot cocoa. Ever tried white chocolate hot cocoa? It's really good!

∽ ∽ ∽

Homemade Hot Cocoa Mix

3 cups Nestle's Quick

8 cups instant dry milk

8 ounces powdered coffee creamer

1/2 cup powdered sugar (or to taste)

2/3 cup Hershey Cocoa

Blend all of the ingredients in a large bowl. To mix a cup, fill your cup with about 1/2 Hot Cocoa Mix and half hot water or to taste.

❧ ❧ ❧

This makes a fun holiday gift! Just put it in a jar with a label and instructions attached. Make sure to make a batch or two for you too. The kids love it with mini marshmallows or whipped cream on top!

❧ ❧ ❧

Chai Latte Mix

1 cup nonfat dry milk powder

2 cups powdered non-dairy creamer

1 package (3.5 ounces) instant vanilla pudding mix

1¼ cups white sugar

1½ cups unsweetened plain instant tea

2 teaspoons ground ginger

2 teaspoons ground cinnamon

1 teaspoon cloves

1/2 teaspoon nutmeg

Combine all ingredients in a very large bowl. Blend this mixture, one cup at a time in a blender or food processor until it›s a fine powder. Stir 2 rounded tablespoons of mix into a mug of very hot water. Makes about 40 servings.

∾ ∾ ∾

I admit it! I love going out for coffee or Chai, but it can really add up! Thanks again Jenn for this homemade chai mix recipe. Now I can make a nice cup of chai at home! All I need is a blanket, a good book, and the dog at my feet. Makes a great gift too!

∾ ∾ ∾

White Wine Sangria

2 bottles (750-ml) dry white wine

1 cup brandy

1/2 cup orange liqueur

1/4 cup superfine sugar (more if you like it sweeter)

1 lime, sliced

1 lemon, sliced

1 orange, sliced

A handful of fresh raspberries or strawberries

Combine the first 4 ingredients in a pitcher and stir well. Add fruit. Chill until ready to serve. Serve over ice.

෨ ෨ ෨

These days you don't need to set up a full bar. Just make a pitcher of this and have the gals over. Set out some snacks like my "Sundried Tomato Dip" and my "Olive Tapenade". Both recipes are in the first chapter. What a great evening! Treasure your girlfriends! I do! We're all in this together!

෨ ෨ ෨

Red Wine Sangria

1 gallon dry red wine

3 oranges, sliced

2 oranges, squeezed

1 lemon, sliced

1 lime sliced

1 apple, sliced

3 tablespoons sugar (more if you like it sweeter)

1/4 cup cointreau or triple sec

1 cup brandy

2 cinnamon sticks

Mix all together, refrigerate at least 4 hours before serving. I like to make it the day before. Taste it to see if more sugar is needed. Serve chilled over ice. You can add other fruit, raspberries, strawberries or mango, if you like.

ᐁ ᐁ ᐁ

I always make this in the summer! It's great for parties or when people just "happen" to stop by. It makes a nice big batch and keep in the fridge for a week.

ᐁ ᐁ ᐁ

Raspberry Lemonade

1 can (12 ounces) frozen lemonade concentrate, thawed

1 bag (12 ounces) frozen raspberries, partially thawed

club soda or sparkling water, chilled

Fresh raspberries

Lemon slices

Fresh mint sprigs

In a blender, puree frozen raspberries. In a pitcher stir together raspberries and lemonade concentrate. Add club soda or sparkling water to taste. Serve in glasses with ice clubs. Garnish with fresh raspberries, lemon slices and fresh mint.

෨ ෨ ෨

This is a really fun summer drink! It's just so pretty and refreshing! Great for showers or summer parties!

෨ ෨ ෨

Cucumber Dill Lemonade

1 English cucumber, peeled and chopped

1/2 cup fresh dill

1 can (12 ounces) frozen lemonade concentrate

1 cup water

Ice

Sparkling water

Gin or vodka (optional)

Fresh cucumber or lemon slices

Blend first four ingredients together until smooth. Pour a little of the mixture over ice and top it off with sparkling water. You can also add vodka or gin for the adults if you'd like. Garnish with lemon slices, cucumber and dill sprigs.

෨ ෨ ෨

I know it sounds like a weird combination but, just try it! On a hot summer day this is just delicious! Everybody loves it. Thanks to a long-time friend and wonderful chef, Susan for this one!

෨ ෨ ෨

That's All Folks!!! For now Anyway!

For more copies of my book, new recipes and information about my favorite aprons and cooking gadgets go to www.thecookingmom.com

I am doing the Twitter and Facebook thing. Find, follow, and friend The Cooking Mom.

I am not the only "Cooking Mom." If you have any great recipes, secrets, or stories let me know about them. We are all in this together. I hope to see you soon. Keep Cooking!

56775665R00201

Made in the USA
Lexington, KY
30 October 2016